BE

MATURE

BE

MATURE

GROWING UP IN CHRIST

NT COMMENTARY

JAMES

Warren W. Wiersbe

David C Cook
transforming lives together

BE MATURE
Published by David C. Cook
4050 Lee Vance View
Colorado Springs, CO 80918 U.S.A.

David C. Cook Distribution Canada
55 Woodslee Avenue, Paris, Ontario, Canada N3L 3E5

David C. Cook U.K., Kingsway Communications
Eastbourne, East Sussex BN23 6NT, England

David C. Cook and the graphic circle C logo
are registered trademarks of Cook Communications Ministries.

LCCN 2008924754
ISBN 978-1-4347-6845-2
eISBN 978-1-4347-6586-4

First edition of *Be Mature* by Warren W. Wiersbe published by Victor Books®
in 1978 © Warren W. Wiersbe, ISBN 978-0-89693-754-3

The Team: Gudmund Lee, Amy Kiechlin, Jack Campbell, and Susan Vannaman
Series Cover Design: John Hamilton Design
Cover Photo: iStockPhoto

Printed in the United States of America
Second Edition 2008

6 7 8 9 10 11 12

020811

Dedicated with love and appreciation to some pastor friends who have been a help and an encouragement to me:

Mark Bubeck
Jerome DeJong
William Larkin
Erwin Lutzer
Douglas Stimers

CONTENTS

THE BIG IDEA

An Introduction to *Be Mature*
by Ken Baugh

Did you know that every carpenter and construction worker has one primary tool that they use more than any other? They use it dozens of times a day and would be lost without it. This tool doesn't require electricity or batteries for it to work, it's not sharp like a saw, and requires very little effort to use. Have you guessed what it is yet? It's a *tape measure*. I'm a carpenter myself and have experience building furniture, framing, and remodeling houses, and I have even built a photography studio, so I know firsthand the importance of a tape measure. Without this simple little tool, you wouldn't be able to make exact cuts—people would have to estimate and make trial cuts that might be close, but never exact. To build anything with any precision requires some type of measuring device like a tape measure.

Did you know that God is a construction worker also? Right now He is building you into the person He wants you to be, using the mold of His Son, Jesus Christ. The theological word for this process is *sanctification*. Others might also refer to this process as "spiritual formation," and that phrase is okay too, but it can be a bit dangerous these days when almost any belief can fall into the category of "spiritual." Therefore, I prefer to use the phrase "Christ-formation" so there is no confusion about the goal of the process. In fact, I believe that Christ-formation is God's primary goal for our lives as His followers, and we see this emphasized over and over again in Scripture: God wants us to be transformed into the image of His Son.

For example, Paul refers to the Christians in Galatia as, "My dear children, for whom I am again in the pains of childbirth until *Christ is formed in you* ..." (Gal. 4:19 NIV). This verse clearly implies this expectation of Christ-formation. Then in 2 Corinthians 3:18 (NIV), Paul emphasizes this fact again by saying, "And we, who with unveiled faces all reflect the Lord's glory, are being *transformed* into his likeness." Christ-formation is God's ultimate goal for every follower of Christ—that slowly, over time, we will begin to think like Jesus, see things as Jesus would see them, and treat people the same as Jesus would treat them. Now don't get me wrong, I don't think that any human being in this life will ever become fully transformed—that won't happen until we get to heaven. But this transformation process *is* supposed to be progressive, meaning that every day we should be more like Jesus than we were yesterday. So here's my question: If God wants us to become more and more like Jesus, which He clearly does, how does this happen? The answer is simple: Scripture. God uses Scripture as a tape measure for the Christ-formation process. The apostle Paul outlines this for us in Romans 12:2: "Do not conform any longer to the pattern of this world, but be transformed by the renewing of your mind." Let me briefly unpack what Paul means here.

When Paul tells us not to *"conform any longer to the pattern of this world,"* he is assuming that we *are* conforming, and he is commanding us to stop. The phrase "be transformed" is an imperative in the Greek text, which means that it is a command. Now, it wouldn't make sense for Paul to command us to do something that we couldn't do, would it? Of course not. Therefore, there must be something that we are able do that facilitates this Christ-formation process. What is it, you ask? Simply this: to study, meditate, memorize, and apply God's Word to our lives.

Think of it like this: Bible study is kind of like going to the gym and working out. When you study your Bible, you are exercising spiritually. We see this analogy over and over again in Scripture. Paul told Timothy: "Spend your time and energy in the exercise of keeping *spiritually fit*" (1 Tim. 4:7 TLB). The Greek word used here for "spiritually fit" is *gymnasia*, which is obviously where we get our English word *gymnasium*. Paul is telling Timothy to exercise himself spiritually, the implication being that spiritual exercise will help him grow strong in his faith and character. Paul goes on to say in verse 8: "Bodily exercise is all right, but *spiritual exercise is much more important* and is a tonic for all you do. So *exercise yourself spiritually*, and practice being a better Christian because that will help you not only now in this life, but in the next life too" (TLB). Peter says the same thing: "… grow in spiritual strength and become better acquainted with our Lord and Savior Jesus Christ" (2 Peter 3:18 TLB).

Spiritual exercises need not be limited to Bible study, as you could also include prayer, fasting, solitude, silence, and a host of others. But the primary activity for transforming the mind is time spent in God's Word. The bottom line is this: If you want to become more and more like Jesus Christ, study, meditate, memorize, and apply the Scriptures to your life. When you begin to take the initiative for this Christ-formation process in your own life, then you will know that you are on the path to spiritual maturity.

Now you might be wondering, what does all of this have to do with the book of James? Here it is: The central theme for the book of James is maturity. God wants us to grow up in our faith, and James tells us how to do it. In fact, about half of the verses in James contain verbs in the imperative form—these are not options, suggestions, or even good ideas, but requirements for Christlike living. For example: "*Consider* it pure joy, my brothers, whenever you face trials of many kinds" (1:2 NIV); "*Do not merely listen* to the word, and so deceive yourselves. *Do* what it says" (1:22 NIV);

"… *don't show favoritism*" (2:1 NIV); "*Submit* yourselves, then, to God. *Resist* the devil …" (4:7 NIV); "*Humble yourselves* before the Lord …" (4:10 NIV); "… *do not slander* one another …" (4:11 NIV); "*Be patient*, then, brothers, until the Lord's coming" (5:7 NIV). The spiritually maturing person takes responsibility to read and follow these commands themselves—they don't need to be spoon fed what they are to do, and they don't blame others when they falter. So, if you want to become strong in your faith and more Christlike in your behavior, you need to take responsibility for your own spiritual growth.

Someone once asked Olympic swimming champion Mark Spitz how he won seven gold medals during the 1972 Summer Olympics. He said it was simple: "I just spent eight hours in the pool a day for four solid years." I think it's easy to admire Olympic athletes as they are racking up their medals during the events. When they stand on the platform to receive their medals we cheer, but what we don't see is the daily routine that each of them had to commit to in order to become a champion. They had to make sacrifices, stay on strict diets, exercise constantly, and make their training a personal mission in life. As you grow and mature in your faith by reading and applying the Word of God to your life, it will have its affect in transforming you more and more into the person of Jesus Christ. And as you read and study through the book of James, let this book be the tape measure that you use to facilitate the exact cuts and changes in your life as you work out your salvation.

***

Dr. Wiersbe's commentaries have been a source of guidance and strength to me over the many years that I have been a pastor. His unique style is not overly academic, but theologically sound. He explains the deep truths of Scripture in a way that everyone can understand and apply. Whether you're a Bible scholar or a brand-new believer in Christ, you will benefit, as I have, from Warren's insights. With your Bible in one hand and Dr. Wiersbe's commentary in the other, you will be able to accurately unpack the deep truths of God's Word and learn how to apply them to your life.

Drink deeply, my friend, of the truths of God's Word, for in them you will find Jesus Christ, and there is freedom, peace, assurance, and joy.

—Ken Baugh
Pastor of Coast Hills Community Church
Aliso Viejo, California

A Word from the Author

Not everybody who grows old, grows up. There is a vast difference between age and maturity. Ideally, the older we are, the more mature we should be; but too often the ideal does not become the real.

The result is problems—problems in personal lives, in homes, and in churches. As a pastor, I see more problems in these areas caused by immaturity than by anything else. If Christians would just grow up, they would become victors instead of victims.

The epistle of James was written to help us understand and attain spiritual maturity: "… that ye may be perfect and entire, wanting nothing" (James 1:4). I like the way J. B. Phillips puts it: "… and you will find you have become men of mature character, men of integrity with no weak spots."

I trust that these simple expository studies will help you reach that goal.

—Warren W. Wiersbe

A SUGGESTED OUTLINE OF THE BOOK OF JAMES

Theme: Spiritual maturity

Key verse: James 1:4

The Marks of the Mature Christian:

I. He is patient in testing (James 1)
    A. Trials on the outside (James 1:1–12)
    B. Temptations on the inside (James 1:13–27)

II. He practices the truth (James 2)
    A. Faith and love (James 2:1–13)
    B. Faith and works (James 2:14–26)

III. He has power over his tongue (James 3)
    A. Exhortation (James 3:1–2)
    B. Illustrations (James 3:3–12)
    C. Application (James 3:13–18)

IV. He is a peacemaker, not a troublemaker (James 4)
    A. Three wars (James 4:1–3)
    B. Three enemies (James 4:4–7)
    C. Three admonitions (James 4:8–17)

V. He is prayerful in troubles (James 5)
    A. Economic troubles (James 5:1–9)
    B. Physical troubles (James 5:10–16)
    C. National troubles (James 5:17–18)
    D. Church troubles (James 5:19–20)

Chapter One

TIME TO GROW UP

(James 1:1)

Beginning a study of a book of the Bible is something like preparing for a trip: You like to know where you are going and what you can expect to see. When my wife and I were getting ready for our first visit to Great Britain, we spent many hours reading travel books and poring over maps. When we arrived there, we enjoyed the visit much more because we knew what we were looking for and how to find it.

Perhaps the best way to launch a study of the epistle of James is to answer four important questions.

1. WHO WAS JAMES?

"James, a servant of God and of the Lord Jesus Christ" (James 1:1a) is the way he introduced himself. It was a popular name, a form of the great Old Testament name "Jacob." There were several men who bore this name in New Testament history.

James, the son of Zebedee and brother of John. He was one of the most prominent to bear the name. He was a fisherman called by Christ to follow and become a disciple (Matt. 4:17–22). He and his brother John were nicknamed by Christ "sons of thunder" because of their impulsiveness

(Mark 3:17; Luke 9:51–56). James was the first of the disciples to give his life for Christ. He was killed by Herod in AD 44 (Acts 12:1–2).

James, the son of Alphaeus. He was another of the disciples (Matt. 10:3; Acts 1:13), but very little is known about him. Matthew (Levi) is also identified as "the son of Alphaeus" (Mark 2:14), and some students conjecture that the two men might have been brothers. There is no indication that this James wrote the letter we are about to study.

James, the father of Judas the disciple. He is an even more obscure man (Luke 6:16, where "brother" ought to be "father"). This Judas was called "the son of James" to distinguish him from Judas Iscariot.

James, the brother of our Lord. He seems to be the most likely candidate for author of this letter. He does not identify himself in this way; humbly, he calls himself "a servant of God and of the Lord Jesus Christ." That Jesus had brothers and sisters is stated in Matthew 13:55–56 and Mark 6:3, and one of His brothers was named James. (By "brother," of course, I mean half-brother. Joseph was not our Lord's father since Jesus was conceived by the Holy Spirit of God.)

James and the other brothers did not believe in Jesus during His earthly ministry (Mark 3:31–35; John 7:1–5). Yet we find our Lord's brethren in the upper room praying with the disciples (Acts 1:14). What effected the change from unbelief to faith? First Corinthians 15:7 indicates that Jesus appeared to James after His resurrection! This convinced James that Jesus truly was the Savior, and he, in turn, shared this knowledge about Jesus with the other brothers.

James became the leader of the church in Jerusalem. Paul called him a pillar in Galatians 2:9. It was James who moderated the church conference described in Acts 15. When Peter was delivered from prison, he sent a special message to James (Acts 12:17); and when Paul visited Jerusalem, it was to James that he brought greetings and the special "love offering" from the Gentiles (Acts 21:18–19).

We have no record in the Bible, but tradition tells us that James was martyred in AD 62. The story is that the Pharisees in Jerusalem so hated James' testimony for Christ that they had him cast down from the temple and then beaten to death with clubs. The story also relates that James died, as did his Savior, praying for his murderers, "Father, forgive them, for they know not what they do."

What kind of a man was James? He must have been a deeply spiritual man to gain the leadership of the Jerusalem church in so short a time. His stature is seen in Acts 15, where he was able to permit all the factions to express themselves, and then bring peace by drawing a conclusion based on the Word of God. Paul, in 1 Corinthians 9:5, suggested that he was a married man. Again, tradition tells us that he was a man of prayer, and this explains the emphasis on prayer in his letter. It was said that he prayed so much, his knees were as hard as a camel's!

James was a Jew, reared in the tradition of the law of Moses, and his Jewish legalism stands out in his letter. (Note also Acts 21:18ff., where James asked Paul to help him pacify the Christian legalists in the Jerusalem church.) There are over fifty imperatives in the epistle of James. James did not suggest—he commanded! He quoted the Old Testament only five times, but there are many allusions to Old Testament passages in the letter.

While still an unbeliever, James must have paid attention to what Jesus taught; in his letter there are numerous allusions to our Lord's sayings, particularly the Sermon on the Mount. Compare these passages:

- James 1:2—Matthew 5:10–12
- James 1:4—Matthew 5:48
- James 1:5—Matthew 7:7–12
- James 1:22—Matthew 7:21–27
- James 4:11–12—Matthew 7:1–5
- James 5:1–3—Matthew 6:19–21

Keep in mind that James led the church in Jerusalem during a very difficult time. It was a time of transition, and such times are always upsetting and demanding. There were many Christian Jews in Jerusalem who still held to the Old Testament law (Acts 21:20). The temple and its services were still in operation, and the full light of the gospel of God's grace had not yet dawned. We who have read Romans, Galatians, and Hebrews might be prone to judge these early believers, but we must not. They were saved people, but they were still in the shadows of the law, moving out into the bright light of God's grace. While there may have been differences in degrees of spiritual knowledge and experience, there was no competition between Paul and those who directed the Jerusalem church (Gal. 2:1–10).

2. TO WHOM DID JAMES WRITE?

"To the twelve tribes which are scattered abroad, greeting" (James 1:1b). James wrote to Jews living outside the land of Palestine. The term "twelve tribes" can only mean the people of Israel, the Jewish nation (Acts 26:7). The fact that many Jews lived outside their Promised Land is evidence of the spiritual decline of the nation. God had to scatter them (Deut. 4:25ff.). When Peter addressed that huge Jewish congregation at Pentecost, he spoke to men from many different nations (Acts 2:9–11).

James sent his letter to *Christian* Jews. At least nineteen times he addressed them as "brethren," indicating not only "brothers in the flesh" (fellow Jews), but also "brothers in the Lord." James was very clear on the doctrine of the new birth (James 1:18). There are times when James also addressed wicked men who were not in the fellowship (the rich, for example, in James 5:1–6), but he did so in order to teach and encourage the saved Jews to whom he sent the letter.

The word *scattered* in James 1:1 is an interesting one. It means "in the dispersion." The term "the dispersion" was used to identify the Jews living outside the land of Palestine. But the Greek word carries the idea of "scattering seed." When the Jewish believers were scattered in that first wave of persecution (Acts 8:1, 4), it was really the sowing of seed in many places; and much of that seed bore fruit (Acts 11:19ff.).

Christian Jews scattered throughout the Roman Empire would have needs and problems of their own. Being Jews, they would be rejected by the Gentiles, and being *Christian* Jews, they would be rejected by their own countrymen. This letter indicates that most of these believers were poor, and some of them were being oppressed by the rich.

3. WHY DID JAMES WRITE?

Each New Testament letter has its own special theme, purpose, and destination. Paul wrote the book of Romans to prepare the Roman Christians for his intended visit. First Corinthians was sent to the church at Corinth to help correct certain problems. Galatians was written to a group of churches to warn them against legalism and false teaching.

As you read the epistle of James, you discover that these Jewish Christians were having some problems in their personal lives and in their church fellowship. For one thing, they were going through difficult testings. They were also facing temptations to sin. Some of the believers were catering to the rich, while others were being robbed by the rich. Church members were competing for offices in the church, particularly teaching offices.

One of the major problems in the church was a failure on the part of many to live what they professed to believe. Furthermore, the tongue was a serious problem, even to the point of creating wars and divisions in the assembly. Worldliness was another problem. Some of the members were disobeying God's Word and were sick physically because of it, and some were straying away from the Lord and the church.

As we review this list of problems, does it appear to be much different from the problems that beset the average local church today? Do we not have in our churches people who are suffering for one reason or another? Do we not have members who talk one way, but walk another way? Is not worldliness a serious problem? Are there not Christians who cannot control their tongues? It seems that James was dealing with very up-to-date matters!

But James was not discussing an array of miscellaneous problems. All of these problems had a common cause: *spiritual immaturity.* These Christians simply were not growing up. This gives us a hint as to the basic theme of this letter: *the marks of maturity in the Christian life.* James used the word *perfect* several times, a word that means "mature, complete" (see James 1:4, 17, 25; 2:22; 3:2). By "a perfect man" (James 3:2) James did not mean a sinless man, but rather one who is mature, balanced, grown-up.

Spiritual maturity is one of the greatest needs in churches today. Too many churches are playpens for babies instead of workshops for adults. The members are not mature enough to eat the solid spiritual food that they need, so they have to be fed on milk (Heb. 5:11–14). Just look at the problems James dealt with and you can see that each of them is characteristic of little children:

- Impatience in difficulties—1:1–4
- Talking but not living the truth—2:14ff.
- No control of the tongue—3:1ff.
- Fighting and coveting—4:1ff.
- Collecting material "toys"—5:1ff.

After well over a quarter century of ministry, I am convinced that spiritual immaturity is the number one problem in our churches. God is looking for mature men and women to carry on His work, and sometimes all He can find are little children who cannot even get along with each other.

The five chapters of this letter suggest the five marks of the mature Christian (see outline).

Of course, this is but one approach to this letter; there are other ways to study it. As the chapters are examined, spiritual maturity and how it may be attained will be emphasized.

The epistle of James logically follows the epistle to the Hebrews, for one of the major themes of Hebrews is *spiritual perfection*. The word *perfect* is found in Hebrews at least fourteen times. The key verse is Hebrews 6:1—"Let us go on unto perfection" meaning, "spiritual maturity." The writer of Hebrews explained the perfect salvation to be had in Christ. James exhorted his readers to build on this perfect salvation and grow into maturity. Without the perfect work of Christ there could be no perfecting of the believers.

How Can We Get the Most Out of This Study?

Since the theme is spiritual maturity, we must begin by examining our own hearts to see where we are in the Christian life.

First of all, it is essential that we have been born again. Apart from spiritual birth there can be no spiritual maturity. James mentioned the new birth early in his letter: "Of his own will begat he us with the word of truth" (James 1:18). The parallel to this is 1 Peter 1:23—"Being born again, not of corruptible seed, but of incorruptible, by the word of God, which liveth and abideth for ever."

Just as a human baby has two parents, so a spiritual baby has two parents—the Word of God and the Spirit of God. We have already quoted two verses that mention the Word of God. John 3:5–6 mentions the Spirit of God. (It is my conviction that "born of water" here refers to physical birth. All babies are "born of water." Nicodemus thought in terms of physical birth in John 3:5.)

How, then, is a person "born again"? The Spirit of God takes the Word of God and generates new life within the heart of the sinner who believes on Jesus Christ. It is a miracle. The Spirit uses the Word to convict the sinner and then to reveal the Savior. We are saved by faith (Eph. 2:8–9), and faith comes from the Word of God (Rom. 10:17).

If we have been born again, there is a second essential for getting the most out of what James has written: We must honestly examine our lives in the light of God's Word. James compares the Bible to a mirror (James 1:22ff.). As we study the Word, we are looking into the divine mirror and seeing ourselves as we really are. But James warns us that we must be honest about what we see and not merely glance at the image and walk away.

Perhaps you heard about the primitive tribesman who looked into a mirror for the first time. He was so shocked at what he saw that he broke the mirror! Many Christians make the same mistake: They criticize the preacher or the lesson, when they ought to be judging themselves.

This leads to a third essential: We must obey what God teaches us, no matter what the cost. We must be "doers of the word and not hearers only" (James 1:22). It is easy to attend a Bible study, share the lesson, and discuss it, but it is much more difficult to go out into life in the workaday world and practice what we have learned. The blessing does not come in *studying* the Word, but in *doing* the Word. Unless we are willing to obey, the Lord is not obligated to teach us (John 7:17).

The fourth essential is that we be prepared for some extra trials and testings. Whenever we are serious about spiritual growth, the enemy gets serious about opposing us. Perhaps you feel a need for more patience. Then be prepared for more trials, because "tribulation worketh patience" (Rom. 5:3). The real examinations in Bible study come in the school of life, not in the classroom.

I know of a man who was burdened to grow in his patience. He knew he was immature in that area of his life, and he wanted to grow up. He sincerely prayed, "Lord, help me to grow in patience. I want to have more self-control in this area of my life." That morning, he missed his train to work and spent the next fifty minutes pacing the platform and complaining of his plight. As the next train to the city arrived, the man realized how stupid he had been. "The Lord gave me nearly an hour to grow in my patience, and all I did was practice my impatience!" he said to himself.

There may come a time in this study when you decide that continuing is too dangerous. Satan may turn on the heat and make things so difficult for you that you will want to retreat. *Don't do it!* When that time arrives, you will be on the verge of a new and wonderful blessing in your own life, a thrilling new step of maturity. Even if Satan does turn on the heat, your Father in heaven keeps His almighty hand on the thermostat!

Even physical maturity is not always an easy, pleasant experience. The teenager walking that difficult bridge from childhood to adulthood has his frustrations and failures, but if he keeps on going (and growing), he eventually enters a wonderful life of maturity. Christian growth is not automatic, as is physical growth. Christian maturity is something we must work at constantly. So don't give up! There is travail in birth, and there is also travail in maturity (Gal. 4:19).

Finally, we must measure our spiritual growth by the Word of God. We should not measure ourselves by other Christians, but by the Word of God and the Son of God (Eph. 4:13). At the close of this study, a dozen questions are listed, based on James, that may help in a personal evaluation. Feel free to turn to them at any time, because regular examinations are good for spiritual health.

Not everyone who grows old, grows up. There is a difference between age and maturity. Just because a Christian has been saved for ten or twenty years does not guarantee that he is mature in the Lord. Mature Christians are happy Christians, useful Christians, Christians who help to encourage others and to build their local church. As we study James together, with God's help we will learn together and mature together.

QUESTIONS FOR PERSONAL REFLECTION
OR GROUP DISCUSSION

1. Who was James? To whom did James write?

2. Why would the early church be identified with "scattered seed"?

3. Why is it important not to retreat in the midst of conflict? How can we prepare ourselves before the conflicts or trials come?

4. What were the main problems of James' readers?

5. What was the common cause of all these problems? What does this mean?

6. What does James mean by the word *perfect*?

7. What are five marks of a mature Christian?

8. How is a person born again?

9. What factors are essential to become spiritually mature?

10. Of these essentials, which is easiest for you? Which is most difficult?

Chapter Two

TURNING TRIALS INTO TRIUMPHS

(James 1:2–12)

Perhaps you have seen the bumper sticker that reads, "When life hands you lemons, make lemonade!" It is easier to smile at that statement than to practice it, but the basic philosophy is sound. In fact, it is biblical. Throughout the Bible are people who turned defeat into victory and trial into triumph. Instead of being victims, they became victors.

James tells us that we can have this same experience today. No matter what the trials may be on the outside (James 1:1–12) or the temptations on the inside (James 1:13–27), through faith in Christ we can experience victory. The result of this victory is spiritual maturity.

If we are going to turn trials into triumphs, we must obey four imperatives: *count* (James 1:2), *know* (James 1:3), *let* (James 1:4, 9–11), and *ask* (James 1:5–8). Or, to put it another way, there are four essentials for victory in trials: a joyful attitude, an understanding mind, a surrendered will, and a heart that wants to believe.

1. COUNT—A JOYFUL ATTITUDE (1:2)

Outlook determines outcome, and attitude determines action. God tells us to *expect trials*. It is not *"if* you fall into various testings" but *"when* you fall into various testings." The believer who expects his Christian life to be easy is in for a shock. Jesus warned His disciples, "In the world ye shall have tribulation" (John 16:33). Paul told his converts that "we must through much tribulation enter into the kingdom of God" (Acts 14:22).

Because we are God's "scattered people" and not God's "sheltered people," we must experience trials. We cannot always expect everything to go our way. Some trials come simply because we are human—sickness, accidents, disappointments, even seeming tragedies. Other trials come because we are Christians. Peter emphasized this in his first letter: "Beloved, think it not strange concerning the fiery trial which is to try you, as though some strange thing happened unto you" (1 Peter 4:12). Satan fights us, the world opposes us, and this makes for a life of battle.

The phrase "fall into" does not suggest a stupid accident. Translate it "encounter, come across." A Christian certainly should not manufacture trials. The Greek word translated "divers" means "various, varicolored." Peter used the same word in 1 Peter 1:6—"Ye are in heaviness through manifold temptations." The trials of life are not all alike; they are like variegated yarn that the weaver uses to make a beautiful rug. God arranges and mixes the colors and experiences of life. The final product is a beautiful thing for His glory.

My wife and I once visited a world-famous weaver and watched his men and women work on the looms. I noticed that the undersides of the rugs were not very beautiful; the patterns were obscure and the loose ends of yarn dangled. "Don't judge the worker or the work by looking at the wrong side," our guide told us. In the same way, we are looking at the wrong side of life; only the Lord sees the finished pattern. Let's not judge Him or His work from what we see today. His work is not finished yet!

The key word is *count.* It is a financial term, and it means "to evaluate." Paul used it several times in Philippians 3. When Paul became a Christian, he evaluated his life and set new goals and priorities. Things that were once important to him became "garbage" in the light of his experience with Christ. When we face the trials of life, we must evaluate them in the light of what God is doing for us.

This explains why the dedicated Christian can have joy in the midst of trials: *He lives for the things that matter most.* Even our Lord was able to endure the cross because of "the joy that was set before him" (Heb. 12:2), the joy of returning to heaven and one day sharing His glory with His church.

Our values determine our evaluations. If we value comfort more than character, then trials will upset us. If we value the material and physical more than the spiritual, we will not be able to "count it all joy." If we live only for the present and forget the future, then trials will make us bitter, not better. Job had the right outlook when he said, "But he knoweth the way that I take: when he hath tried me, I shall come forth as gold" (Job 23:10).

So, when trials come, immediately give thanks to the Lord and adopt a joyful attitude. Do not pretend; do not try self-hypnosis; simply look at trials through the eyes of faith. Outlook determines outcome; to *end* with joy, *begin* with joy.

"But how," we may ask, "is it possible to rejoice in the midst of trials?" The second imperative explains this.

2. Know—an Understanding Mind (1:3)

What do Christians know that makes it easier to face trials and benefit from them?

Faith is always tested. When God called Abraham to live by faith, He tested him in order to increase his faith. God always tests us to bring out the *best;* Satan tempts us to bring out the worst. The testing of our faith proves that we are truly born again.

Testing works for us, not against us. The word *trying* can be translated "approval." Again, Peter helps us understand it better: "That the trial of your faith, being much more precious than of gold that perisheth" (1 Peter 1:7). A gold prospector brings his ore sample into the assayer's office to be tested. The sample itself may not be worth more than a few dollars, but the *approval*—the official statement about the ore—is worth millions! It assures the prospector that he has a gold mine. God's approval of our faith is precious, because it assures us that our faith is genuine.

Trials work *for* the believer, not *against* him. Paul said, "And we know that all things work together for good" (Rom. 8:28), and, "For our light affliction, which is but for a moment, worketh for us a far more exceeding and eternal weight of glory" (2 Cor. 4:17).

Trials rightly used help us to mature. What does God want to produce in our lives? Patience, endurance, and the ability to keep going when things are tough. "We glory in tribulations also: knowing that tribulation worketh patience; and patience, experience; and experience, hope" (Rom. 5:3–4). In the Bible, *patience* is not a passive acceptance of circumstances. It is a courageous perseverance in the face of suffering and difficulty.

Immature people are always impatient; mature people are patient and persistent. Impatience and unbelief usually go together, just as faith and patience do. "Be ... followers of them who through faith and patience inherit the promises" (Heb. 6:12). "For ye have need of patience, that, after ye have done the will of God, ye might receive the promise" (Heb. 10:36). "He that believeth shall not make haste" (Isa. 28:16).

God wants to make us patient because that is the key to every other blessing. The little child who does not learn patience will not learn much of anything else. When the believer learns to wait on the Lord, then God can do great things for him. Abraham ran ahead of the Lord, married Hagar, and brought great sorrow into his home (Gen. 16). Moses ran ahead of God, murdered a man, and had to spend forty years with the sheep to learn patience (Ex. 2:11ff.). Peter almost killed a man in his impatience (John 18:10–11).

The only way the Lord can develop patience and character in our lives is through trials. Endurance cannot be attained by reading a book (even this one), listening to a sermon, or even praying a prayer. We must go through the difficulties of life, trust God, and obey Him. The result will be patience and character. Knowing this, we can face trials joyfully. We know what trials will do in us and for us, and we know that the end result will bring glory to God.

This fact explains why studying the Bible helps us grow in patience (Rom. 15:4). As we read about Abraham, Joseph, Moses, David, and even our Lord, we realize that God has a purpose in trials. God fulfills His purposes as we trust Him. There is no substitute for an understanding mind. Satan can defeat the ignorant believer, but he cannot overcome the Christian who knows his Bible and understands the purposes of God.

3. LET—A SURRENDERED WILL (1:4, 9–12)

God cannot build our character without our cooperation. If we resist Him, then He chastens us into submission. But if we submit to Him, then He can accomplish His work. He is not satisfied with a halfway job. God wants a perfect work; He wants a finished product that is mature and complete.

God's goal for our lives is maturity. It would be a tragedy if our children remained little babies. We enjoy watching them mature, even though maturity brings dangers as well as delights. Many Christians shelter themselves from the trials of life, and as a result, never grow up. God wants the "little children" to become "young men," and the "young men" He wants to become "fathers" (1 John 2:12–14).

Paul outlined three works that are involved in a complete Christian life

(Eph. 2:8–10). First, there is the work God does *for us,* which is salvation. Jesus Christ completed this work on the cross. If we trust Him, He will save us. Second, there is the work God does *in us:* "For we are his workmanship." This work is known as *sanctification:* God builds our character and we become more like Jesus Christ, "conformed to the image of his Son" (Rom. 8:29). The third work is what God does *through us*—service. We are "created in Christ Jesus unto good works."

God builds character before He calls to service. He must work *in* us before He can work *through* us. God spent twenty-five years working in Abraham before He could give him his promised son. God worked thirteen years in Joseph's life, putting him into "various testings" before He could put him on the throne of Egypt. He spent eighty years preparing Moses for forty years of service. Our Lord took three years training His disciples, building their character.

But God cannot work in us without our consent. There must be a surrendered will. The mature person does not argue with God's will; instead, he accepts it willingly and obeys it joyfully. "Doing the will of God from the heart" (Eph. 6:6). If we try to go through trials without surrendered wills, we will end up more like immature children than mature adults.

Jonah is an illustration of this. God commanded Jonah to preach to the Gentiles at Nineveh, and he refused. God chastened Jonah before the prophet accepted his commission. But Jonah did not obey God from the heart. He did not grow in this experience. How do we know? Because in the last chapter of Jonah, the prophet is acting like a spoiled child! He is sitting outside the city pouting, hoping that God will send judgment. He is impatient with the sun, the wind, the gourd, the worm, and with God.

One difficult stage of maturing is *weaning.* A child being weaned is sure that his mother no longer loves him and that everything is against him. Actually, weaning is a step toward maturity and liberty. It is good for the child! Sometimes God has to wean His children away from their childish toys and immature attitudes. David pictured this in Psalm 131: "Surely I have behaved and quieted myself, as a child that is weaned of his mother: my soul is even as a weaned child" (v. 2). God uses trials to wean us away from childish things; but if we do not surrender to Him, we will become even more immature.

In James 1:9–11, James applied this principle to two different kinds of Christians: the poor and the rich. Apparently, money and social status were real problems among these people (see James 2:1–7, 15–16; 4:1–3, 13–17; 5:1–8). *God's testings have a way of leveling us.* When testing comes to the poor man, he lets God have His way and rejoices that he possesses spiritual riches that cannot be taken from him. When testing comes to the rich man, he also lets God have His way, and he rejoices that his riches in Christ cannot wither or fade away. In other words, it is not your material resources that take you through the testings of life; it is your spiritual resources.

We have three imperatives from James so far: *count*—a joyful attitude; *know*—an understanding heart; *let*—a surrendered will. He gives a fourth.

4. ASK—A BELIEVING HEART (1:5–8)

The people to whom James wrote had problems with their praying (James 4:1–3; 5:13–18). When we are going through God-ordained difficulties, what should we pray about? James gives the answer: Ask God for *wisdom.*

James has a great deal to say about wisdom (James 1:5; 3:13–18). The Jewish people were lovers of wisdom, as the book of Proverbs gives evidence. Someone has said that knowledge is the ability to take things apart, while wisdom is the ability to put them together. Wisdom is the right use of knowledge. All of us know people who are educated fools: They have brilliant academic records, but they cannot make the simplest decisions in life. I once met a gifted professor on a seminary campus, and he was wearing two hats!

Why do we need wisdom when we are going through trials? Why not ask for strength, or grace, or even deliverance? For this reason: *We need wisdom so we will not waste the opportunities God is giving us to mature.* Wisdom helps us understand how to use these circumstances for our good and God's glory.

An associate of mine, a gifted secretary, was going through great trials. She had had a stroke, her husband had gone blind, and then he had to be taken to the hospital where (we were sure) he would die. I saw her in church one Sunday and assured her that I was praying for her.

"What are you asking God to do?" she asked, and her question startled me.

"I'm asking God to help you and strengthen you," I replied.

"I appreciate that," she said, "but pray about one more thing. Pray that I'll have the wisdom not to waste all of this!"

She knew the meaning of James 1:5.

James not only explained *what* to ask for (wisdom), but he also described *how* to ask. We are to ask in faith. We do not have to be afraid, for God is anxious to answer, and He will never scold us! "He giveth more grace" (James 4:6). He also gives more and more wisdom. The greatest enemy to answered prayer is unbelief.

James compares the doubting believer to the waves of the sea, up one minute and down the next. While vacationing in Hawaii, I learned that you cannot trust the waves. I was sitting on a rock by the ocean, watching the waves and enjoying the sunshine. I heard a sound behind me, turned to see who was approaching, and instantly was drenched by a huge wave! Never turn your back on the waves—they are down, then they are up.

This is the experience of the "double-minded man." Faith says, "Yes!"

but unbelief says, "No!" Then doubt comes along and says "Yes!" one minute and "No!" the next. It was doubt that made Peter sink in the waves as he was walking to Jesus (Matt. 14:22–33). Jesus asked him, "O thou of little faith, wherefore didst thou doubt?" When Peter started his walk of faith, he kept his eyes on Christ. But when he was distracted by the wind and waves, he ceased to walk by faith, and he began to sink. He was double-minded, and he almost drowned.

Many Christians live like corks on the waves: up one minute, down the next; tossed back and forth. This kind of experience is evidence of immaturity. Paul used a similar idea in Ephesians 4:14—"That we henceforth be no more children, tossed to and fro, and carried about with every wind of doctrine, by the sleight of men, and cunning craftiness, whereby they lie in wait to deceive." If we have believing and united hearts, we can ask in faith and God will give the wisdom we need. Instability and immaturity go together.

James closed this section with a beatitude: "Blessed is the man that endureth temptation" (James 1:12). He started (James 1:2) and ended with joy. Outlook determines outcome. This beatitude is a great encouragement because it promises a crown to those who patiently endure trials. Paul often used athletic illustrations in his letters, and James did so here. He is not saying that the sinner is saved by enduring trials. He is saying that the believer is rewarded by enduring trials.

How is he rewarded? First, by growth in Christian character. This is more important than anything else. He is rewarded also by bringing glory to God and by being granted a crown of life when Jesus Christ returns. First the cross, then the crown. First the suffering, then the glory. God does not help us by removing the tests, but by making the tests work for us. Satan wants to use the tests to tear us down, but God uses them to build us up.

In James 1:12, James used a very important word: *love*. We would expect him to write, "the crown of life, which the Lord hath promised to them that trust Him" or "that obey Him." Why did James use *love?* Because love is the spiritual motivation behind every imperative in this section.

Why do we have a joyful attitude as we face trials? Because we love God, and He loves us, and He will not harm us. Why do we have an understanding mind? Because He loves us and has shared His truth with us, and we love Him in return. Why do we have a surrendered will? Because we love Him. Where there is love, there is surrender and obedience. Why do we have a believing heart? Because love and faith go together. When you love someone, you trust him, and you do not hesitate to ask him for help.

Love is the spiritual force behind the imperatives James gave us. If we love God, we will have no problem counting, knowing, letting, and asking. But there is another factor involved: Love keeps us faithful to the Lord. The double-minded person (James 1:8) is like an unfaithful husband or wife: He wants to love both God and the world. James admonished, "Purify your hearts, ye double-minded!" (James 4:8). The Greek word translated "purify" literally means "make chaste." The picture is that of an unfaithful lover.

Let's go back to the weaning. The child who loves his mother, and who is sure that his mother loves him, will be able to get through the weaning and start to grow up. The Christian who loves God, and who knows that God loves him, will not fall apart when God permits trials to come. *He is secure in God's love.* He is not double-minded, trying to love both God and the world. Lot was double-minded; when trials came, he failed miserably. Abraham was the friend of God; he loved God and trusted Him. When trials came, Abraham triumphed and matured in the faith.

God's purpose in trials is maturity. "Let patience have her perfect work, that yc may be perfect and entire, wanting nothing." The Charles B. Williams translation says it graphically: "But you must let your endurance come to its perfect product so that you may be fully developed and perfectly equipped."

If that is what you want, then in love to Christ, *count, know, let,* and *ask*!

QUESTIONS FOR PERSONAL REFLECTION
OR GROUP DISCUSSION

1. What are four essential elements for victory in trials?

2. What relationship exists between a person's values and his or her attitude toward trials?

3. Why can dedicated Christians have joy in the midst of trials?

4. How would you define patience?

5. Why do you think Wiersbe states that patience is the key to every other
blessing? What part does the Bible play in growing patience?

6. What is God's goal for us as Christians?

7. How do Abraham, Joseph, Moses, and the disciples illustrate the "sanctification before service" principle?

8. What is God's spiritual weaning process? How does James 1:9–11 illustrate this?

9. When faced with a trial, what should you pray and how should you pray?

10. In James 1:12, what relationship do you see between enduring temptation and loving the Lord?

Chapter Three

How to Handle Temptation

(James 1:13–18)

The mature person is patient in trials. Sometimes the trials are testings on the outside, and sometimes they are temptations on the inside. Trials may be tests sent by God, or they may be temptations sent by Satan and encouraged by our own fallen nature. It is this second aspect of trials—temptations on the inside—that James dealt with in this section.

We may ask, "Why did James connect the two? What is the relationship between testings without and temptations within?" Simply this: If we are not careful, the testings on the outside may become temptations on the inside. When our circumstances are difficult, we may find ourselves complaining against God, questioning His love, and resisting His will. At this point, Satan provides us with an opportunity to escape the difficulty. This opportunity is a temptation.

There are many illustrations of this truth found in the Bible. Abraham arrived in Canaan and discovered a famine there. He was not able to care for his flocks and herds. This trial was an opportunity to prove God; but Abraham turned it into a temptation and went down to Egypt. God had to chasten Abraham to bring him back to the place of obedience and blessing.

While Israel was wandering in the wilderness, the nation often turned testings into temptations and tempted the Lord. No sooner had they been delivered from Egypt than their water supply vanished and they had to march for three days without water. When they did find water, it was so bitter they could not drink it. Immediately they began to murmur and blame God. They turned their testing into a temptation, and they failed.

Certainly, God does not want us to yield to temptation, yet neither can He spare us the experience of temptation. We are not God's *sheltered* people; we are God's *scattered* people. If we are to mature, we must face testings and temptations. There are three facts that we must consider if we are to overcome temptation.

1. Consider God's Judgment (1:13–16)

This is a negative approach, but it is an important one. James said, "Look ahead and see where sin ends—death!" Do not blame God for temptation. He is too holy to be tempted, and He is too loving to tempt others. God does test us, as He did Abraham (Gen. 22); but He does not and cannot tempt us. It is we who turn occasions of testing into temptations.

A temptation is an opportunity to accomplish a good thing in a bad way, out of the will of God. Is it wrong to want to pass an examination? Of course not, but if you cheat to pass it, then you have sinned. The temptation to cheat is an opportunity to accomplish a good thing (passing the examination) in a bad way. It is not wrong to eat, but if you consider stealing the food, you are tempting yourself.

We think of sin as a single act, but God sees it as a process. Adam committed one act of sin, and yet that one act brought sin, death, and judgment on the whole human race. James described this process of sin in four stages.

(1) Desire (v. 14). The word *lust* means any kind of desire, and not necessarily sexual passions. The normal desires of life were given to us by

God and, of themselves, are not sinful. Without these desires, we could not function. Unless we felt hunger and thirst, we would never eat and drink, and we would die. Without fatigue, the body would never rest and would eventually wear out. Sex is a normal desire; without it the human race could not continue.

It is when we want to satisfy these desires in ways outside God's will that we get into trouble. Eating is normal; gluttony is sin. Sleep is normal; laziness is sin. "Marriage is honorable in all, and the bed undefiled: but whoremongers and adulterers God will judge" (Heb. 13:4).

Some people try to become "spiritual" by denying these normal desires or by seeking to suppress them, but this only makes them less than human. These fundamental desires of life are the steam in the boiler that makes the machinery go. Turn off the steam and you have no power. Let the steam go its own way and you have destruction. The secret is in *constant control.* These desires must be our servants and not our masters, and this we can do through Jesus Christ.

(2) Deception (v. 14). No temptation appears as temptation; it always seems more alluring than it really is. James used two illustrations from the world of sports to prove his point. *Drawn away* carries with it the idea of the baiting of a trap; and *enticed* in the original Greek means "to bait a hook." The hunter and the fisherman have to use bait to attract and catch their prey. No animal is deliberately going to step into a trap and no fish will knowingly bite at a naked hook. The idea is to *hide* the trap and the hook.

Temptation always carries with it some bait that appeals to our natural desires. The bait not only attracts us, but it also hides the fact that yielding to the desire will eventually bring sorrow and punishment. It is the bait that is the exciting thing. Lot would never have moved toward Sodom had he not seen the "well-watered plains of Jordan" (Gen. 13:10ff.). When David looked on his neighbor's wife, he would never have committed adultery had he seen the tragic consequences: the death of a baby (Bathsheba's son), the murder of a brave soldier (Uriah), the violation of a daughter (Tamar). *The bait keeps us from seeing the consequences of sin.*

When Jesus was tempted by Satan, He always dealt with the temptation on the basis of the Word of God. Three times He said, "It is written." From the human point of view, turning stones into bread to satisfy hunger is a sensible thing to do; but not from God's point of view. When you know the Bible, you can detect the bait and deal with it decisively. This is what it means to walk by faith and not by sight.

(3) Disobedience (v. 15). We have moved from the *emotions* (desire) and the *intellect* (deception) to the *will*. James changed the picture from hunting and fishing to the birth of a baby. Desire conceives a method for taking the bait. The will approves and acts, and the result is sin. Whether we feel it or not, we are hooked and trapped. The baby is born, and just wait until it matures!

Christian living is a matter of the will, not the feelings. I often hear believers say, "I don't feel like reading the Bible." Or, "I don't feel like attending prayer meeting." Children operate on the basis of feeling, but adults operate on the basis of will. *They act because it is right, no matter how they feel.* This explains why immature Christians easily fall into temptation: They let their feelings make the decisions. The more you exercise your will in saying a decisive no to temptation, the more God will take control of your life. "For it is God which worketh in you both to will and to do of his good pleasure" (Phil. 2:13).

(4) Death (v. 15). Disobedience gives birth to death, not life. It may take years for the sin to mature, but when it does, the result will be death. If we will only believe God's Word and see this final tragedy, it will encourage us not to yield to temptation. God has erected this barrier because He loves us. "Have I any pleasure at all that the wicked should die?" (Ezek. 18:23).

These four stages in temptation and sin are perfectly depicted in the first sin recorded in the Bible in Genesis 3.

The serpent used *desire* to interest Eve: "For God doth know that in the day ye eat thereof, then your eyes shall be opened, and ye shall be as gods, knowing good and evil" (Gen. 3:5). Is there anything wrong with gaining knowledge? Is there anything wrong with eating food? Eve saw that "the tree was good for food" (Gen. 3:6), and her desire was aroused.

Paul described the deception of Eve in 2 Corinthians 11:3: "But I fear, lest by any means, as the serpent beguiled Eve through his subtlety, so your minds should be corrupted from the simplicity that is in Christ." Satan is the deceiver, and he seeks to deceive the mind. The bait that he used with Eve was the fact that the forbidden tree was good and pleasant, and that eating of it would make her wise. She saw the bait but forgot the Lord's warning: "In the day that thou eatest thereof thou shalt surely die" (Gen. 2:17).

Eve disobeyed God by taking the fruit of the tree and eating it. Then she shared it with her husband, and he disobeyed God. Because Adam was not deceived, but sinned with his eyes wide open, it is his sin that plunged the human race into tragedy (read Rom. 5:12–21; 1 Tim. 2:12–15).

Both Adam and Eve experienced immediate spiritual death (separation from God) and ultimate physical death. All men die because of Adam (1 Cor. 15:21–22). The person who dies without Jesus Christ will experience eternal death, the lake of fire (Rev. 20:11–15).

Whenever you are faced with temptation, get your eyes off the bait and look ahead to see the consequences of sin: *the judgment of God.* "For the wages of sin is death" (Rom. 6:23).

2. CONSIDER GOD'S GOODNESS (1:17)

One of the enemy's tricks is to convince us that our Father is holding out on us, that He does not really love us and care for us. When Satan

approached Eve, he suggested that if God really loved her, He would permit her to eat of the forbidden tree. When Satan tempted Jesus, he raised
the question of hunger: "If Your Father loves You, why are You hungry?"

The goodness of God is a great barrier against yielding to temptation.
Since God is good, we do not need any other person (including Satan) to
meet our needs. It is better to be hungry *in* the will of God than full *outside* the will of God. Once we start to doubt God's goodness, we will be
attracted to Satan's offers, and the natural desires within will reach out for
his bait. Moses warned Israel not to forget God's goodness when they began
to enjoy the blessings of the Promised Land (Deut. 6:10–15). We need this
warning today. James presented four facts about the goodness of God.

(1) God gives only good gifts. Everything good in this world comes
from God. If it did not come from God, it is not good. If it comes from
God, it must be good, even if we do not see the goodness in it immediately.
Paul's thorn in the flesh was given to him by God and it seemed to be a
strange gift; yet it became a tremendous blessing to him (2 Cor. 12:1–10).

(2) The way God gives is good. We can translate the second clause
"and every act of giving." It is possible for someone to give us a gift in a
manner that is less than loving. The value of a gift can be diminished by the
way it is given to us. But when God gives us a blessing, He does it in a loving, gracious manner. *What* He gives and *how* He gives are both good.

(3) He gives constantly. "Cometh down" is a present participle: It
keeps on coming down. God does not give occasionally; He gives constantly. Even when we do not see His gifts, He is sending them. How do we
know this? Because He tells us so and we believe His Word.

(4) God does not change. There are no shadows with the Father of
Lights. It is impossible for God to change. He cannot change for the worse
because He is holy; He cannot change for the better because He is already
perfect. The light of the sun varies as the earth changes, but the sun itself is

still shining. If shadows come between us and the Father, He did not cause them. He is the unchanging God. This means that we should never question His love or doubt His goodness when difficulties come or temptations appear.

If King David had remembered the goodness of the Lord, he would not have taken Bathsheba and committed those terrible sins. At least this is what Nathan the prophet told the king. "Thus saith the LORD God of Israel, I anointed thee king over Israel, and I delivered thee out of the hand of Saul; and I gave thee thy master's house, and thy master's wives into thy bosom, and gave thee the house of Israel and of Judah; and if that had been too little, I would moreover have given unto thee such and such things" (2 Sam. 12:7–8). Note the repetition of the word *give* in this brief statement. God had been good to David, yet David forgot God's goodness and took the bait.

The first barrier against temptation is a negative one: the judgment of God. This second barrier is positive: the goodness of God. A fear of God is a healthy attitude, but the love of God must balance it. We can obey Him because He may chasten us, or we can obey Him because He has already been so generous to us, and because we love Him for it.

It was this positive attitude that helped to keep Joseph from sinning when he was tempted by his master's wife (Gen. 39:7ff.). "Behold, with me here, my master does not concern himself with anything in the house, and he has put all that he owns in my charge. There is no one greater in this house than I, and he has withheld nothing from me except you, because you are his wife. How then could I do this great evil and sin against God?" (Gen. 39:8–9 NASB). Joseph knew that all these blessings had come from God. It was the goodness of God, through the hands of his employer, that restrained him in the hour of temptation.

God's gifts are always better than Satan's bargains. Satan never gives any gifts, because you end up *paying for them dearly.* "It is the blessing of the LORD that makes rich, and He adds no sorrow to it" (Prov. 10:22 NASB). Achan forgot the warning of God and the goodness of God, saw the forbidden wealth, coveted it, and took it. He became rich, but the sorrow that followed turned his riches into poverty (Josh. 7).

The next time you are tempted, meditate on the goodness of God in your life. If you think you need something, wait on the Lord to provide it. Never toy with the Devil's bait. One purpose for temptation is to teach us patience. David was tempted twice to kill King Saul and hasten his own coronation, but he resisted the temptation and waited for God's time.

3. CONSIDER GOD'S DIVINE NATURE WITHIN (1:18)

In the first barrier, God says, "Look ahead and beware of judgment." In the second barrier, He says, "Look around and see how good I have been to you." But with this third barrier, God says, "Look within and realize that you have been born from above and possess the divine nature."

James used birth as a picture of desire leading to sin and death (James 1:15). He also used it to explain how we can enjoy victory over temptation and sin. The apostle John used a similar approach in 1 John 3:9, where "his seed" refers to the divine life and nature within the believer. Note the characteristics of this birth.

It is divine. Nicodemus thought he had to reenter his mother's womb to be born again, but he was wrong. This birth is not of the flesh; it is from above (John 3:1–7). It is the work of God. Just as we did not generate our own human birth, we cannot generate our own spiritual birth. When we put our faith in Jesus Christ, it was God who performed the miracle.

It is gracious. We did not earn it or deserve it; God gave us spiritual birth because of His own grace and will. "Which were born, not of blood [human descent], nor of the will of the flesh [human efforts], nor of the will of man [human assistance], but of God" (John 1:13). No one can be born again because of his relatives, his resolutions, or his religion. The new birth is the work of God.

It is through God's Word. Just as human birth requires two parents, so divine birth has two parents: the Word of God and the Spirit of God. "That which is born of the flesh is flesh; and that which is born of the Spirit is spirit" (John 3:6). "Being born again, not of corruptible seed, but of incorruptible, by the word of God, which liveth and abideth forever" (1 Peter 1:23). The Spirit of God uses the Word of God to bring about the miracle of the new birth. Since the Word of God is "living and powerful" (Heb. 4:12), it can generate life in the heart of the sinner who trusts Christ, and that life is God's life.

It is the finest birth possible. We are "a kind of firstfruits of his creatures," James wrote to Jewish believers, and the word *firstfruits* would be meaningful to them. The Old Testament Jews brought the firstfruits to the Lord as the expression of their devotion and obedience. "Honour the LORD with thy substance, and with the firstfruits of all thine increase" (Prov. 3:9). Of all the creatures God has in this universe, Christians are the very highest and the finest! We share God's nature. For this reason, it is beneath our dignity to accept Satan's bait or to desire sinful things. A higher birth must mean a higher life.

By granting us a new birth, God declares that He cannot accept the old birth. Throughout the Bible, God rejects the firstborn and accepts the secondborn. He accepted Abel, not Cain; Isaac, not Ishmael; Jacob, not Esau. He rejects your first birth (no matter how noble it might have been in the eyes of men), and He announces that you need a second birth.

It is this experience of the new birth that helps us overcome temptation. If we let the old nature (from the first birth) take over, we will fail. We received our old nature (the flesh) from Adam, and he was a failure. But if we yield to the new nature, we will succeed, for that new nature comes from Christ, and He is the Victor.

A Sunday school child explained the matter in simple terms. "Two men live in my heart: the old Adam and Jesus. When temptation knocks at the door, somebody has to answer. If I let Adam answer, I will sin, *so I send Jesus to answer.* He always wins!"

Of course, this new nature must be fed the Word of God daily, that it might be strong to fight the battle. Just as the Holy Spirit used the Word of God to give you spiritual birth, He uses the Word to give you spiritual strength. "Man shall not live by bread alone, but by every word that proceedeth out of the mouth of God" (Matt. 4:4).

No matter what excuses we make, we have no one to blame for sin but ourselves. Our own desires lead us into temptation and sin. God is not to blame. But God has erected these three barriers to keep us from sin. If we heed the barriers, we will win a crown (James 1:12). If we break through the barriers, we will find a coffin (James 1:15). Which will it be?

QUESTIONS FOR PERSONAL REFLECTION
OR GROUP DISCUSSION

1. What is the distinction between testing on the outside and temptation on the inside?

2. What must we understand if we are to overcome temptation?

3. What are the four stages of the process of sin? How are these four stages depicted in Genesis 3? How can you relate to them personally?

4. Why do immature Christians so easily fall into temptations? What should we do when faced with temptations?

5. What pictures help us understand the meaning of *drawn away* and *enticed?*

6. What does James teach us about the goodness of God?

7. What are three barriers against temptation? Which are you most likely to forget?

8. What are four characteristics of the divine new birth?

9. Who are the two "parents" of the divine birth? Why could these be thought of as "parents"?

10. What excuses might Christians make for yielding to sin? Why is each invalid?

Chapter Four

QUIT KIDDING YOURSELF

(James 1:19–27)

The emphasis in this section is on the dangers of self-deception: "deceiving your own selves" (James 1:22); "deceiveth his own heart" (James 1:26). If a Christian sins because Satan deceives him, that is one thing. But if he deceives himself, that is a far more serious matter.

Many people are deceiving themselves into thinking they are saved when they are not. "Many will say to me in that day, Lord, Lord, have we not prophesied in thy name? and in thy name have cast out devils? and in thy name done many wonderful works? And then will I profess unto them, I never knew you: depart from me, ye that work iniquity" (Matt. 7:22–23).

But there are true believers who are fooling themselves concerning their Christian walk. They think they are spiritual when they are not. It is a mark of maturity when a person faces himself honestly, knows himself, and admits his needs. It is the immature person who pretends, "I am rich, and increased with goods, and have need of nothing" (Rev. 3:17).

Spiritual reality results from the proper relationship to God through His Word. God's Word is truth (John 17:17), and if we are rightly related to God's truth, we cannot be dishonest or hypocritical. In these verses,

James stated that we have three responsibilities toward God's Word, and if we fulfill these responsibilities, we will have an honest walk with God and men.

1. RECEIVE THE WORD (1:19–21)

James called God's Word "the engrafted word" (James 1:21), which means "the implanted word." Borrowing from our Lord's parable of the sower (Matt. 13:1–9, 18–23), he compared God's Word to seed and the human heart to soil. In His parable, Jesus described four kinds of hearts: *the hard heart,* which did not understand or receive the Word and therefore bore no fruit; *the shallow heart,* which was very emotional but had no depth and bore no fruit; *the crowded heart,* which lacked repentance and permitted sin to crowd out the Word; and *the fruitful heart,* which received the Word, allowed it to take root, and produced a harvest of fruit.

The final test of salvation is fruit. This means a changed life, Christian character and conduct, and ministry to others in the glory of God. This fruit might be winning souls to Christ (Rom. 1:16), growing in holy living (Rom. 6:22), sharing our material possessions (Rom. 15:28), spiritual character (Gal. 5:22–23), good works (Col. 1:10), and even praising the Lord (Heb. 13:15). Religious works may be manufactured, but they do not have life in them, nor do they bring glory to God. Real fruit has in it the seed for more fruit, so that the harvest continues to grow fruit, more fruit, much fruit (John 15:1–5).

But the Word of God cannot work in our lives unless we receive it in the right way. Jesus not only said, "Take heed what ye hear" (Mark 4:24), but He also said, "Take heed how ye hear" (Luke 8:18). Too many people are in that tragic condition in which "hearing they hear not, neither do they understand" (Matt. 13:13). They attend Bible classes and church services but never seem to grow. Is it the fault of the teacher or the preacher?

Perhaps, but it may also be the fault of the hearer. It is possible to be "dull of hearing" (Heb. 5:11) because of decay of the spiritual life.

If the seed of the Word is to be planted in our hearts, then we must obey the instructions James gave us.

Swift to hear (v. 19a). "Who hath ears to hear, let him hear" (Matt. 13:9)! "So then faith cometh by hearing, and hearing by the word of God" (Rom. 10:17). Just as the servant is quick to hear his master's voice, and the mother to hear her baby's smallest cry, so the believer should be quick to hear what God has to say.

There is a beautiful illustration of this truth in the life of King David (2 Sam. 23:14–17). David was hiding from the Philistines who were in possession of Bethlehem. He yearned for a drink of the cool water from the well in Bethlehem, a well that he had often visited in his boyhood and youth. He did not issue an order to his men; he simply said to himself, "Oh, that one would give me drink of the water of the well of Bethlehem, which is by the gate" (2 Sam. 23:15). Three of his mighty men heard their king sigh for the water, and they risked their lives to secure the water and bring it to him. They were "swift to hear."

Slow to speak (v. 19b). We have two ears and one mouth, which ought to remind us to listen more than we speak. Too many times we argue with God's Word, if not audibly, at least in our hearts and minds. "He that refraineth his lips is wise" (Prov. 10:19). "He that hath knowledge spareth his words" (Prov. 17:27). Instead of being slow to speak, the lawyer in Luke 10:29 argued with Jesus by asking, "And who is my neighbor?" In the early church, the services were informal, and often the listeners would debate with the speaker. There were even fightings and wars among the brethren James was writing to (James 4:1).

Slow to wrath (v. 19c). Do not get angry at God or His Word. "He that is slow to wrath is of great understanding: but he that is hasty of spirit exalteth folly" (Prov. 14:29). When the prophet Nathan told King David the story about "the stolen ewe lamb," the king became angry, but at the wrong person. "Thou art the man," said Nathan, and David then confessed, "I have sinned" (2 Sam. 12). In the garden, Peter was slow to hear, swift to speak, and swift to anger—and he almost killed a man with the sword. Many church fights are the result of short tempers and hasty words. There is a godly anger against sin (Eph. 4:26), and if we love the Lord, we must hate sin (Ps. 97:10). But man's anger does not produce God's righteousness (James 1:20). In fact, anger is just the opposite of the patience God wants to produce in our lives as we mature in Christ (James 1:3–4).

I once saw a poster that read, "Temper is such a valuable thing, it is a shame to lose it!" It is temper that helps to give steel its strength. The person who cannot get angry at sin does not have much strength to fight it. James warns us against getting angry at God's Word because it reveals our sins to us. Like the man who broke the mirror because he disliked the image in it, people rebel against God's Word because it tells the truth about them and their sinfulness.

A prepared heart (v. 21). James saw the human heart as a garden; if left to itself, the soil would produce only weeds. He urged us to "pull out the weeds" and prepare the soil for the "implanted Word of God." The phrase "superfluity of naughtiness" gives the picture of a garden overgrown with weeds that cannot be controlled. It is foolish to try to receive God's Word into an unprepared heart.

How do we prepare the soil of our hearts for God's Word? First, by confessing our sins and asking the Father to forgive us (1 John 1:9). Then, by meditating on God's love and grace and asking Him to "plow up" any hardness in our hearts: "Break up your fallow ground, and sow not among thorns" (Jer. 4:3). Finally, we must have an attitude of "meekness" (James 1:21). Meekness is the opposite of "wrath" in James 1:19–20. When you receive the Word with meekness, you accept it, do not argue with it, and honor it as the Word of God. You do not try to twist it to conform it to your thinking.

If we do not receive the implanted Word, then we are deceiving ourselves. Christians who like to argue various "points of view" may be only fooling themselves. They think that their "discussions" are promoting spiritual growth, when in reality they may only be cultivating the weeds.

2. PRACTICE THE WORD (1:22–25)

It is not enough to hear the Word; we must do it. Many people have the mistaken idea that hearing a good sermon or Bible study is what makes them grow and get God's blessing. It is not the hearing but *the doing* that brings the blessing. Too many Christians mark their Bibles, but their Bibles never mark them! If you think you are spiritual because you hear the Word, then you are only kidding yourself.

In the previous paragraph, James compared the Word to seed, but in this paragraph, he compared it to a mirror. There are two other references in the Bible to God's Word as a mirror; and when you put all three together, you discover three ministries of the Word of God as a mirror.

(1) Examination (vv. 23–25). This is the main purpose for owning a mirror, to be able to see yourself and make yourself look as clean and neat as possible. As we look into the mirror of God's Word, we see ourselves as we really are. James mentions several mistakes people make as they look into God's mirror.

First, *they merely glance at themselves.* They do not carefully study themselves as they read the Word. Many sincere believers read a chapter of the Bible each day, but it is only a religious exercise and they fail to profit from it personally. Their conscience would bother them if they did not have their daily reading, when actually their conscience should bother them *because they read the Word carelessly.* A cursory reading of the Bible will never reveal our deepest needs. It is the difference between a candid photo and an X-ray.

The second mistake is that *they forget what they see.* If they were looking deeply enough into their hearts, what they would see would be unforgettable! We tend to smile at the "extremes" of people back in the days of the great revivals, but perhaps we could use some of that conviction. John Wesley wrote about a preaching service: "One before me dropped as dead, and presently a second, and a third. Five others sunk down in half an hour, most of whom were in violent agonies" (*Wesley's Journal* for June 22, 1739). Before we consign these people to some psychological limbo, remember how saints in the Bible responded to the true knowledge of their own hearts. Isaiah cried, "Woe is me! for I am undone" (Isa. 6:5)! Peter cried, "Depart from me, for I am a sinful man, O Lord" (Luke 5:8)! Job was the most righteous man on earth in his day, yet he confessed, "I abhor myself, and repent in dust and ashes" (Job 42:6).

Mistake number three: *they fail to obey what the Word tells them to do.* They think that *hearing* is the same as *doing,* and it is not. We Christians enjoy substituting *reading* for *doing,* or even *talking* for *doing.* We hold endless committee meetings and conferences about topics like evangelism and church growth, and think we have made progress. While there is certainly nothing wrong with conferences and committee meetings, they are sinful if they are a substitute for service.

If we are to use God's mirror profitably, then we must gaze into it carefully and with serious intent (James 1:25). No quick glances will do. We must examine our own hearts and lives in the light of God's Word. This requires time, attention, and sincere devotion. Five minutes with God each day will never accomplish a deep spiritual examination.

I have been fortunate with the doctors who have cared for me through the years, and I owe a great deal to them. Each of them has possessed two qualities that I have appreciated: They have spent time with me and have not been in a hurry, and they have always told me the truth. When Jesus, the Great Physician (Matt. 9:12), examines us, He uses His Word, and He wants us to give Him sufficient time to do the job well. Perhaps one reason we glance into the Word instead of gaze into the Word is that we are afraid of what we might see.

After seeing ourselves, we must remember what we are and what God says, and we must *do the Word*. The blessing comes in the doing, not in the reading of the Word. "This man shall be blessed in his doing" (James 1:25, literal translation). The emphasis in James is on the practice of the Word. We are to *continue* after reading the Word (James 1:25; see Acts 1:14; 2:42, 46; 13:43; 14:22; 26:22 for examples of this in the early church).

Why did James call the Word of God "the perfect law of liberty" (James 1:25)? Because when we obey it, God sets us free. "And I will walk at liberty: for I seek thy precepts" (Ps. 119:45). "Whosoever committeth sin is the servant of sin" (John 8:34). "If ye continue in my word, then are ye my disciples indeed; and ye shall know the truth, and the truth shall make you free" (John 8:31–32).

But *examination* is but the first ministry of the mirror of the Word. There is a second ministry.

(2) Restoration (Ex. 38:8). When he built the tabernacle, Moses took the metal looking glasses of the women and from them made the laver. The laver was a huge basin that stood between the brazen altar of sacrifice and the holy place. (Read Ex. 30:17–21 for details.) The basin was filled with water, and the priests washed their hands and feet at the laver before they entered the holy place to minister.

Water for washing is a picture of the Word of God in its cleansing power. "Now ye are clean through the word which I have spoken unto you" (John 15:3). The church is sanctified and cleansed "with the washing of water by the word" (Eph. 5:26). When the sinner trusts Christ, he is once and for all washed clean (1 Cor. 6:9–11; Titus 3:4–6). But as the believer walks in this world, his hands and feet are defiled, and he needs cleansing (John 13:1–11).

The mirror of the Word not only examines us and reveals our sins, but it helps to cleanse us as well. It gives us the promise of cleansing (1 John 1:9) and, as we meditate on it, it cleanses the heart and the mind from spiritual defilement. It is the blood of Christ that cleanses the guilt, but the water of the Word helps to wash away the defilement.

Nathan's experience with David in 2 Samuel 12 helps to illustrate this truth. Nathan told David the story about the stolen ewe lamb, and David became angry at the sin described. "Thou art the man," said the prophet, and he held up the mirror of the Word for David to see himself. The result was confession and repentance: "I have sinned against the Lord!" The mirror of the Word did its work of examination.

But Nathan did not stop there. He also used the Word for *restoration*. "The Lord also hath put away thy sin; thou shalt not die" (2 Sam. 12:13). Here was the assurance of forgiveness and cleansing, and it came from the Word. David visited the laver and washed his hands and feet.

If we stop with examination and restoration, we will miss the full benefit of the mirror ministry of the Word. There is a third ministry.

(3) Transformation (2 Cor. 3:18). After the Lord restores us, He wants to change us so that we will grow in grace and not commit that sin again. Too many Christians confess their sins and claim forgiveness, but never grow spiritually to conquer self and sin.

Second Corinthians 3 is a discussion of the contrasts between the old covenant ministry of law and the new covenant ministry of grace. The law is external, written on tablets of stone; but salvation means that God's Word is written on the heart. The old covenant ministry condemned and killed; but the new covenant ministry brings forgiveness and life. The glory of the law gradually disappeared, but the glory of God's grace becomes brighter and brighter. The law was temporary, but the new covenant of grace is eternal.

Paul's illustration of this truth is Moses and his veil. When Moses came down from the mount where he met God, his face was shining (Ex. 34:29–35). He did not want the Jews to see this glory fading away, so he put on a veil to hide it. When he returned to the mount, he took off the veil. When Jesus died, the veil in the temple was torn from top to bottom, and the veil between men and God was removed. The Old Testament prophet wore a veil to hide the fading of the glory. The New Testament believer has an unveiled face, and the glory gets greater and greater!

You may explain 2 Corinthians 3:18 in this way: "When the child of God looks into the Word of God [the glass, the mirror], he sees the Son of God, and he is transformed by the Spirit of God to share in the glory of God!" The word *changed* in the Greek gives us our English word *metamorphosis*—a change on the outside that comes from the inside. When an ugly worm turns into a beautiful butterfly, this is metamorphosis. When a believer spends time looking into the Word and seeing Christ, he is transformed: The glory on the inside is revealed on the outside.

It is this word that is translated "transfigured" in Matthew 17:2. The glory of Christ on the mount was not reflected; it was radiated from within. You will find the same word in Romans 12:2: "Be ye transformed by the renewing of your mind." As we meditate on the Word, the Spirit renews the mind and reveals the glory of God. We do not become spiritual Christians overnight. It is a process, the work of the Spirit of God through the mirror of the Word of God.

The important thing is that we hide nothing. Take off the veil! "Search me, O God, and know my heart: try me, and know my thoughts:

and see if there be any wicked way in me, and lead me in the way ever-lasting" (Ps. 139:23–24). "If we say that we have no sin, we deceive ourselves, and the truth is not in us" (1 John 1:8).

Our first responsibility is to receive the Word. Then, we must prac-tice the Word; otherwise we are deceiving ourselves. This leads to a third responsibility.

3. SHARE THE WORD (1:26–27)

The word translated "religion" means "the outward practice, the service of a god." It is used only five times in the entire New Testament (James 1:26–27; Acts 26:5; and Col. 2:18, where it is translated "worshipping"). Pure reli-gion has nothing to do with ceremonies, temples, or special days. Pure religion means practicing God's Word and sharing it with others, through speech, service, and separation from the world.

Speech (v. 26). There are many references to speech in this letter, giv-ing the impression that the tongue was a serious problem in the assembly (see James 1:19; 2:12; 3:1–3, 14–18; 4:11–12). It is the tongue that reveals the heart (Matt. 12:34–35); if the heart is right, the speech will be right. A controlled tongue means a controlled body (James 3:1ff.).

Service (v. 27a). After we have seen ourselves and Christ in the mirror of the Word, we must see others and their needs. Isaiah first saw the Lord, then himself, and then the people to whom he would minister (Isa. 6:1–8). Words are no substitute for deeds of love (James 2:14–18; 1 John 3:11–18). God does not want us to pay for others to minister as a substitute for our own personal service!

Separation from the world (v. 27b). By "the world" James meant "society without God." Satan is the prince of this world (John 14:30), and the lost are the children of this world (Luke 16:8). As the children of God, we are *in* the world physically but not *of* the world spiritually

(John 17:11–16). We are sent *into* the world to win others to Christ (John 17:18). It is only as we maintain our separation from the world that we can serve others.

The world wants to "spot" the Christian and start to defile him. First, there is "friendship of the world" (James 4:4), which can lead to a love for the world (1 John 2:15–17). If we are not careful, we will become conformed to this world (Rom. 12:1–2), and the result is being condemned with the world (1 Cor. 11:32). This does not suggest that we lose our salvation, but that we lose all we have lived for. Lot is an illustration of this principle. First he pitched his tent toward Sodom, and then he moved into Sodom. Before long, Sodom moved into him and he lost his testimony even with his own family. When judgment fell on Sodom, Lot lost everything. It was Abraham, the separated believer, the friend of God, who had a greater ministry to the people than did Lot, the friend of the world. It is not necessary for the Christian to get involved with the world to have a ministry to the world. Jesus was "unspotted" (1 Peter 1:19), and yet He was the friend of publicans and sinners. The best way to minister to the needs of the world is to be pure from the defilement of the world.

QUESTIONS FOR PERSONAL REFLECTION
OR GROUP DISCUSSION

1. What is the role of God's Word for seeing spiritual reality?

2. What are our responsibilities toward God's Word?

3. What is the final test of salvation? What might this look like in a believer's life?

4. Since religious works can be manufactured and untrue, how can we know the difference between these and true good works?

5. How can we prepare our hearts to receive God's Word?

6. In what ways is God's Word a mirror?

7. What mistakes do Christians sometimes make when they look into God's mirror?

8. What often gets substituted for doing the Word? Why do you think this happens?

9. What ministries does the mirror of the Word have?

10. What is pure religion? Why must we be separated from or unstained by the world?

Chapter Five

RICH MAN, POOR MAN

(James 2:1–13)

Not only is the mature Christian patient in testing (James 1), but he also practices the truth. This is the theme of James 2. Immature people talk about their beliefs, but the mature person lives his faith. Hearing God's Word (James 1:22–25) and talking about God's Word can never substitute for doing God's Word.

Every believer has some statement of faith or personal expression of what he believes. Most churches have such statements and members are asked to subscribe to the statement and practice it. Most churches also have a "covenant" that they read publicly, often when they observe the Lord's Supper. Statements of faith and church covenants are good and useful, but they are not substitutes for doing God's will. As a pastor, I have heard believers read the church covenant and then come to a business meeting and act in ways completely contrary to the covenant.

James wanted to help us practice God's Word, so he gave us a simple test. He sent two visitors to a church service, a rich man and a poor man, and he watched to see how they were treated. *The way we behave toward people indicates what we really believe about God!* We cannot—and dare not—separate *human* relationships from *divine* fellowship. "If a man say, I love God, and hateth his brother, he is a liar: for he that loveth not his brother whom he hath seen, how can he love God whom he hath not seen?" (1 John 4:20).

In this section, James examined four basic Christian doctrines in the light of the way we treat other people.

1. THE DEITY OF CHRIST (2:1–4)

"My brothers, don't hold the faith of our Lord Jesus Christ, the Lord of Glory, by showing favoritism" (literal translation). Jewish people in that day coveted recognition and honor, and vied with one another for praise. Our Lord's parables in Luke 14:7–14 deal with the problem, and also His denunciation of the Pharisees in Matthew 23.

We have this same problem with us today. Pyramid climbers are among us, not only in politics, industry, and society, but also in the church. Almost every church has its cliques, and often, new Christians find it difficult to get in. Some church members use their offices to enhance their own images of importance. Many of the believers James wrote to were trying to seize spiritual offices, and James had to warn them (James 3:1).

Jesus did not respect persons. Even His enemies admitted, "You aren't swayed by men, because you pay no attention to who they are" (Matt. 22:16 NIV). Our Lord did not look at the outward appearance; He looked at the heart. He was not impressed with riches or social status. The poor widow who gave her mite was greater in His eyes than the rich Pharisee who boastfully gave his large donation. Furthermore, He saw the potential in the lives of sinners. In Simon, He saw a rock. In Matthew, the publican, He saw a faithful disciple who would one day write one of the four gospels. The disciples were amazed to see Jesus talking with the sinful woman at the well of Sychar, but Jesus saw in her an instrument for reaping a great harvest.

We are prone to judge people by their past, not their future. When Saul of Tarsus was converted, the church in Jerusalem was afraid to receive him! It took Barnabas, who believed in Saul's conversion, to break down the walls (Acts 9:26–28). We are also prone to judge by outward appearance rather than by the inner attitude of the heart. We do not enjoy sitting with certain people in church because they "are not our kind of people." Jesus was the friend of sinners, though He disapproved of their sins. It was not compromise, but compassion, that caused Him to welcome them, and when they trusted Him, forgive them.

Jesus was despised and rejected. This fact was prophesied in Isaiah 53:1–3. He was "the poor man" who was rejected by the self-righteous nation. Unlike the foxes and the birds, He had no home. He grew up in the despised city of Nazareth in a home that knew the feeling of poverty. Had you and I met Him while He was ministering on earth, we would have seen nothing physically or materially that would attract us.

Yet, *He is the very glory of God!* In the Old Testament, God's glory dwelled first in the tabernacle (Ex. 40:34–38) and then in the temple (1 Kings 8:10–11). When Jesus came to earth, God's glory resided in Him (John 1:14). Today, the glory of God dwells in the believer individually (1 Cor. 6:19–20) and the church collectively (Eph. 2:21–22).

The religious experts in Christ's day judged Him by their human standards, and they rejected Him. He came from the wrong city, Nazareth of Galilee. He was not a graduate of their accepted schools. He did not have the official approval of the people in power. He had no wealth. His followers were a nondescript mob and included publicans and sinners. *Yet He was the very glory of God!* No wonder Jesus warned the religious leaders, "Stop judging by mere appearances, and make a right judgment" (John 7:24 NIV).

Sad to say, we often make the same mistakes. When visitors come into our churches, we tend to judge them on what we see outwardly rather than what they are inwardly. Dress, color of skin, fashion, and other superficial things carry more weight than the fruit of the Spirit that may be manifest in their lives. We cater to the rich because we hope to get something out of them, and we avoid the poor because they embarrass us. Jesus did not do this, and He cannot approve of it.

How do we practice the deity of Christ in our human relationships? It is really quite simple: *Look at everyone through the eyes of Christ.* If the visitor is a Christian, we can accept him because *Christ lives in him.* If he is not a Christian, we can receive him because *Christ died for him.* It is Christ who is the link between us and others, and He is a link of love. The basis for relationship with others is the person and work of Jesus Christ. Any other basis is not going to work. Furthermore, God can use even the most unlikely person to bring glory to His name. He used Peter and Zacchaeus and John Mark, and He can use that poor man whom we might reject.

2. THE GRACE OF GOD (2:5–7)

The emphasis here is on God's *choosing,* and this involves the grace of God. If salvation were on the basis of merit, it would not be by grace. Grace implies God's sovereign choice of those who cannot earn and do not deserve His salvation (Eph. 1:4–7; 2:8–10). God saves us completely on the basis of the work of Christ on the cross and not because of anything that we are or have.

God ignores *national* differences (Acts 10:34). The Jewish believers were shocked when Peter went to the Gentile household of Cornelius, preached to the Gentiles, and even ate with them. The topic of the first church council was "Must a Gentile become a Jew to become a Christian?" (Acts 15). The answer the Holy Spirit gave them was "No!" In the sight of God, there is no difference between Jew and Gentile when it comes to condemnation (Rom. 2:6–16) or salvation (Rom. 10:1–13).

God also ignores *social* differences. Masters and slaves (Eph. 6:9) and rich and poor are alike to Him. James taught us that the grace of God makes the rich man poor, because he cannot depend on his wealth; and it makes the poor man rich, because he inherits the riches of grace in Christ. (Review James 1:9–11.) "The LORD maketh poor, and maketh rich: he bringeth low, and lifteth up. He raiseth up the poor out of the dust, and lifteth up the beggar from the dunghill, to set them among princes, and to make them inherit the throne of glory" (1 Sam. 2:7–8).

From the human point of view, God chooses the poor instead of the rich. "For ye see your calling, brethren, how that not many wise men after the flesh, not many mighty, not many noble, are called: but God hath chosen the foolish things of the world to confound the wise; and God hath chosen the weak things of the world to confound the things which are mighty" (1 Cor. 1:26–27). The poor of this world become rich in faith; as sons of God, they inherit the wealth of the kingdom.

It is possible to be poor in this world and rich in the next, or rich in this world and poor in the next (1 Tim. 6:17–18). Or, you could be poor both in this world and the next, or rich in this world and the next. It all depends on what you do with Christ and the material wealth He has given you. God promises the kingdom to "those that love him" (James 2:5), not to those who love this world and its riches.

James gave a stern rebuke in James 2:6–7: "When you despise the poor man, you are behaving like the unsaved rich people." In that day, it was easy for rich persons to exploit the poor, influence decisions at court, and make themselves richer. Unfortunately, we have the same sins being committed today; and these sins blaspheme the very name of Christ. Our Lord was poor, and He too was the victim of injustice perpetrated by the wealthy leaders of His day.

The doctrine of God's grace, if we really believe it, forces us to relate to people on the basis of God's plan and not on the basis of human merit or social status. A "class church" is not a church that magnifies the grace of God. When He died, Jesus broke down the wall that separated Jews and Gentiles (Eph. 2:11–22). But in His birth and life, Jesus broke down the walls between rich and poor, young and old, educated and uneducated. It is wrong for us to build those walls again; we cannot rebuild them if we believe in the grace of God.

3. THE WORD OF GOD (2:8–11)

In recent years, believers have waged battles over the inspiration and author-ity of the Word of God. Certainly, it is a good thing to defend the truth of God's Word, but we must never forget that *our lives and ministries are the best defense.* D. L. Moody often said, "Every Bible should be bound in shoe leather!"

James reached back into the Old Testament for one of God's laws, "Thou shalt love thy neighbor as thyself" (Lev. 19:18). In His parable of the good Samaritan, Jesus told us that our neighbor is anyone who needs our help (Luke 10:25–37). It is not a matter of geography, but opportunity. The important question is not "Who is my neighbor?" but "To whom can I be a neighbor?"

Why is "love thy neighbor" called "the royal law"? For one thing, it was given by the King. God the Father gave it in the law, and God the Son reaf-firmed it to His disciples (John 13:34). God the Spirit fills our hearts with God's love and expects us to share it with others (Rom. 5:5). True believers are "taught of God to love one another" (1 Thess. 4:9).

But "love thy neighbor" is the royal law for a second reason: *It rules all the other laws.* "Love is the fulfilling of the law" (Rom. 13:10). There would be no need for the thousands of complex laws if each citizen truly loved his neighbors.

But the main reason why this is the royal law is that *obeying it makes you a king*. Hatred makes a person a slave, but love sets us free from self-ishness and enables us to reign like kings. Love enables us to obey the Word of God and treat people as God commands us to do. We obey His law, not out of fear, but out of love.

Showing respect of persons can lead a person into disobeying all of God's law. Take any of the Ten Commandments and you will find ways of breaking it if you respect a person's social or financial status. Respect of persons could make you lie, for example. It could lead to idolatry (getting money out of the rich) or even mistreatment of one's parents. Once we start acting on the basis of respecting persons and rejecting God's Word, we are heading for trouble. And we need not break *all* of God's law to be guilty. There is only one Lawgiver, and all of His laws are from His mind and heart. If I disobey one law, I am capable of disobeying all of them; and by rebelling, I have already done so.

Christian love does not mean that I must *like* a person and agree with him on everything. I may not like his vocabulary or his habits, and I may not want him for an intimate friend. *Christian love means treating others the way God has treated me.* It is an act of the will, not an emotion that I try to manufacture. The motive is to glorify God. The means is the power of the Spirit within ("for the fruit of the Spirit is love"). As I act in love toward another, I may find myself drawn more and more to him, and I may see in him (through Christ) qualities that before were hidden to me.

Also, Christian love does not leave the person where it finds him. Love should help the poor man do better; love should help the rich man make better use of his God-given resources. Love always builds up (1 Cor. 8:1); hatred always tears down.

We only believe as much of the Bible as we practice. If we fail to obey the most important word—"love thy neighbor as thyself"—then we will not do any good with the lesser matters of the Word. It was a glaring fault in the Pharisees that they were careful about the minor matters and careless about the fundamentals (Matt. 23:23). They broke the very law they thought they were defending!

4. THE JUDGMENT OF GOD (2:12–13)

Every orthodox statement of faith ends with a statement about the return of Jesus Christ and the final judgment. Not all Christians agree as to the details of these future events, but the certainty of them none denies. Nor would any deny the importance of a final judgment. Both Jesus (John 5:24) and Paul (Rom. 8:1) assured us that Christian believers will never be judged for their sins, but our works will be judged and rewarded (Rom. 14:10–13; 2 Cor. 5:9–10).

Our words will be judged. Note the words spoken to the two visitors in James 2:3. What we say to people, and how we say it, will come up before God. Even our careless words will be judged (Matt. 12:36). Of course, the words we speak come from the heart; so when God judges the words, He is examining the heart (Matt. 12:34–37). Jesus emphasized caution when speaking in some of His warnings in the Sermon on the Mount (Matt. 5:21–26, 33–37; 7:1–5, 21–23).

Our deeds will be judged. Read Colossians 3:22–25 for additional insight. It is true that God remembers our sins against us no more (Jer. 31:34; Heb. 10:17), *but our sins affect our character and works.* We cannot sin lightly and serve faithfully. God forgives our sins when we confess them to Him, but He cannot change their consequences.

Our attitudes will be judged (v. 13). James contrasted two attitudes: showing mercy to others, and refusing to show mercy. If we have been merciful toward others, God can be merciful toward us. However, we must not twist this truth into a lie. It does not mean that we *earn* mercy by showing mercy, because it is impossible to earn mercy. If it is earned, it is not mercy! Nor does it mean that we should "be soft on sin" and never judge it in the lives of others. "I don't condemn anybody," a man once told me, "and God won't condemn me." How wrong he was!

Mercy and justice both come from God, so they are not competitors. Where God finds repentance and faith, He is able to show mercy; where He finds rebellion and unbelief, He must administer justice. It is the heart of the sinner that determines the treatment he gets. Our Lord's parable in Matthew 18:21–35 illustrates the truth. The parable is not illustrating salvation, but forgiveness between fellow servants. If we forgive our brothers, then we have the kind of heart that is open toward the forgiveness of God.

We shall be judged "by the law of liberty." Why did James use this title for God's law? For one thing, when we obey God's law, it frees us from sin and enables us to walk in liberty (Ps. 119:45). Also, *law prepares us for liberty.* A child must be under rules and regulations because he is not mature enough to handle the decisions and demands of life. He is given *outward discipline* so that he might develop *inward discipline,* and one day be free of rules.

Liberty does not mean license. License (doing whatever I want to do) is the worst kind of bondage. Liberty means the freedom to be all that I can be in Jesus Christ. License is confinement; liberty is fulfillment.

Finally, the Word is called "the law of liberty" because God sees our hearts and knows what we would have done had we been free to do so. The Christian student who obeys only because the school has rules is not really maturing. What will he do when he leaves the school? God's Word can change our hearts and give us the desire to do God's will, so that we obey from inward compulsion and not outward constraint.

There is one obvious message to this section: Our beliefs should control our behavior. If we really believe that Jesus is the Son of God, and that

God is gracious, His Word is true, and one day He will judge us, then our conduct will reveal our convictions. Before we attack those who do not have orthodox doctrine, we must be sure that we practice the doctrines we defend. Jonah had wonderful theology, but he hated people and was angry with God (Jonah 4).

One of the tests of the reality of our faith is how we treat other people. Can we pass the test?

QUESTIONS FOR PERSONAL REFLECTION
OR GROUP DISCUSSION

1. What is it about certain people that makes it difficult for you to associate with them?

2. What are some issues that divide some people but are not a problem for you?

3. How does James 2 compare to 1 John 4:20?

4. What does it mean to look at people through the eyes of Christ?

5. On what basis do we tend to judge people? How does Jesus see people?

6. How is God's grace manifested to us in the way He relates to people? How can we imitate this?

7. How is it possible that two commandments can sum up all the law and prophets? Why can love be commanded of us?

8. What are the motive and the means to loving others as God wants us to?

9. What aspects of our behavior toward other people will God judge? By what criteria will God judge?

10. How does showing mercy to others affect God's judgment of us?

Chapter Six

FALSE FAITH

(James 2:14–26)

F aith is a key doctrine in the Christian life. The sinner is saved by faith (Eph. 2:8–9), and the believer must walk by faith (2 Cor. 5:7). Without faith it is impossible to please God (Heb. 11:6), and whatever we do apart from faith is sin (Rom. 14:23).

Someone has said that faith is not "believing in spite of evidence, but obeying in spite of consequence." When you read Hebrews 11, you meet men and women who acted on God's Word, no matter what price they had to pay. Faith is not some kind of nebulous feeling that we work up; faith is confidence that God's Word is true and conviction that acting on that Word will bring His blessing.

In this paragraph, James discussed the relationship between faith and works. This is an important discussion, for if we are wrong in this matter, we jeopardize our eternal salvation. What kind of faith really saves a person? Is it necessary to perform good works in order to be saved? How can a person tell whether or not he is exercising true saving faith? James answered these questions by explaining to us that there are three kinds of faith, only one of which is true saving faith.

1. Dead Faith (2:14–17)

Even in the early church there were those who claimed they had saving faith, yet did not possess salvation. Wherever there is the true, you will find the counterfeit. Jesus warned, "Not every one that saith unto me, Lord, Lord, shall enter into the kingdom of heaven; but he that doeth the will of my Father which is in heaven" (Matt. 7:21).

People with dead faith substitute words for deeds. They know the correct vocabulary for prayer and testimony, and can even quote the right verses from the Bible, but their walk does not measure up to their talk. They think that their words are as good as works, and they are wrong.

James gave a simple illustration. A poor believer came into a fellowship, without proper clothing and in need of food. The person with dead faith noticed the visitor and saw his needs, but he did not do anything to meet the needs. All he did was say a few pious words! "Go, I wish you well; keep warm and well fed" (James 2:16 NIV). But the visitor went away just as hungry and naked as he came in!

Food and clothing are basic needs of every human being, whether he is saved or unsaved. "And having food and raiment let us be therewith content" (1 Tim. 6:8). "Therefore take no thought, saying, What shall we eat? or, What shall we drink? or, Wherewithal shall we be clothed? … for your heavenly Father knoweth that ye have need of all these things" (Matt. 6:31–32). Jacob included these basic needs in his prayer to God: "If God will be with me … and will give me bread to eat, and raiment to put on" (Gen. 28:20).

As believers, we have an obligation to help meet the needs of people, no matter who they may be. "As we have therefore opportunity, let us do good unto all men, especially unto them who are of the household of faith" (Gal. 6:10). "Inasmuch as ye have done it unto one of the least of these my brethren, ye have done it unto me" (Matt. 25:40).

To help a person in need is an expression of love, and faith works by love (Gal. 5:6). The apostle John emphasized this aspect of good works. "If anyone has material possessions and sees his brother in need but has no pity on him, how can the love of God be in him? Dear children, let us not love with words or tongue but with actions and truth" (1 John 3:17–18 NIV). The priest and Levite in the parable of the good Samaritan each had religious training, but neither of them paused to assist the dying man at the side of the road (Luke 10:25–37). Each of them would *defend* his faith, yet neither *demonstrated* that faith in loving works.

The question in James 2:14 should read, "Can *that kind of faith* save him?" What kind? The kind of faith that is never seen in practical works. The answer is no! Any declaration of faith that does not result in a changed life and good works is a false declaration. That kind of faith is dead faith. "Even so faith, if it hath not works, is dead, being alone" (James 2:17). The great theologian John Calvin wrote, "It is faith alone that justifies, but faith that justifies can never be alone." The word *alone* in James 2:17 simply means "by itself." True saving faith can never be by itself: It always brings life, and life produces good works.

The person with dead faith has only an intellectual experience. In his mind, he knows the doctrine of salvation, but he has never submitted himself to God and trusted Christ for salvation. He knows the right words, but he does not back up his words with his works. Faith in Christ brings life (John 3:16), and where there is life there must be growth and fruit. Three times in this paragraph, James warned us that "faith without works is dead" (James 2:17, 20, 26).

Beware of a mere intellectual faith. No man can come to Christ by faith and remain the same any more than he can come into contact with a 220-volt wire and remain the same. "He that hath the Son hath life; and he that hath not the Son of God hath not life" (1 John 5:12). Dead faith is not saving faith. Dead faith is counterfeit faith and lulls the person into a false confidence of eternal life.

2. DEMONIC FAITH (2:18–19)

James wanted to shock his complacent readers, so he used demons as his illustration. In recent years the church has rediscovered the reality and activity of demons. When our Lord was ministering on earth, He often cast out demons, and He gave that power to His disciples. Paul often confronted demonic forces in his ministry, and in Ephesians 6:10–20, he admonished the early Christians to claim God's protection and defeat the spiritual forces of wickedness.

It comes as a shock to people that demons have faith! What do they believe? For one thing, they believe in the existence of God; they are neither atheists nor agnostics. They also believe in the deity of Christ. Whenever they met Christ when He was on earth, they bore witness to His sonship (Mark 3:11–12). They believe in the existence of a place of punishment (Luke 8:31), and they also recognize Jesus Christ as the Judge (Mark 5:1–13). They submit to the power of His Word.

"Hear, O Israel: The LORD our God is one LORD" (Deut. 6:4). This was the daily affirmation of faith of the godly Jew. "You believe that there is one God. Good! Even the demons believe that—and shudder" (James 2:19 NIV). The man with dead faith was touched only in his intellect, but the demons are touched *also in their emotions*. They believe and tremble.

But it is not a saving experience to believe and tremble. A person can be enlightened in his mind and even stirred in his heart and be lost forever. True saving faith involves something more, something that can be seen and recognized: a changed life. "Show me thy faith without thy works," challenged James, "and I will show thee my faith by my works" (James 2:18).

How could a person show his faith without works? Can a dead sinner perform good works? Impossible! When you trust Christ, you are "created in Christ Jesus unto good works, which God hath before ordained that we should walk in them" (Eph. 2:10). Being a Christian involves trusting Christ and living for Christ; you *receive* the life, then you *reveal* the life. Faith that is barren is not saving faith. The Greek word translated "dead" in James 2:20 carries the meaning of "barren or idle," like money drawing no interest.

James has introduced us to two kinds of faith that can never save the sinner: dead faith (the intellect alone) and demonic faith (the intellect and the emotions). He closes this section by describing the only kind of faith that can save the sinner—dynamic faith.

3. DYNAMIC FAITH (2:20–26)

Dynamic faith is faith that is real, faith that has power, faith that results in a changed life.

James *described* this true saving faith. To begin with, dynamic saving faith is *based on the Word of God*. We receive our spiritual rebirth through God's Word (James 1:18). We receive the Word and this saves us (James 1:21). "So then faith cometh by hearing, and hearing by the Word of God" (Rom. 10:17). James used Abraham and Rahab as illustrations of dynamic saving faith, since both of them heard and received the message of God through His Word.

Faith is only as good as its object. The man in the jungle bows before an idol of stone and trusts it to help him, but he receives no help. No matter how much faith a person may generate, if it is not directed at the right object, it will accomplish nothing. "I believe" may be the testimony of many sincere people, but the big question is, "In whom do you believe? What do you believe?" We are not saved by *faith in faith;* we are saved by faith in Christ as revealed in His Word.

Dynamic faith is based on God's Word, and *it involves the whole person*. Dead faith touches only the intellect; demonic faith involves both the mind and the emotions; but dynamic faith involves the will. The whole person plays a part in true saving faith. The mind understands the truth; the heart desires the truth; and the will acts upon the truth. The men and women of faith named in Hebrews 11 were people of action: God spoke and they obeyed. Again, faith is not believing in spite of evidence; faith is obeying in spite of consequence.

True saving faith *leads to action*. Dynamic faith is not intellectual contemplation or emotional consternation; it leads to obedience on the part of the will. And this obedience is not an isolated event: It continues throughout the whole life. It leads to works.

Many different kinds of works are named in the New Testament. "The works of the law" (Gal. 2:16) relate to the sinner's attempt to please God by obeying the law of Moses. Of course, it is impossible for a sinner to be saved through the works of the law. "The works of the flesh" (Gal. 5:19) are done by unsaved people who live for the things of the old nature. There are also "wicked works" (Col. 1:21) and "dead works" (Heb. 9:14). Where there is dynamic faith—saving faith—you will always find good works.

James then *illustrated* his doctrine in the lives of two well-known Bible persons: Abraham and Rahab. You could not find two more different persons! Abraham was a Jew; Rahab was a Gentile. Abraham was a godly man, but Rahab was a sinful woman, a harlot. Abraham was the friend of God, while Rahab belonged to the enemies of God. What did they have in common? Both exercised saving faith in God.

You will want to read Genesis 15 and 22 to get the background facts for this illustration. God called Abraham out of Ur of the Chaldees to lead him into Canaan and to make out of him the great nation of Israel. It was through Israel that God would bring the Savior into the world. Abraham's salvation experience is recorded in Genesis 15. At night, God showed His servant the stars and gave him a promise: "So shall thy seed [descendants] be!" How did Abraham respond? "And he believed in the LORD, and he [the Lord] counted it to him for righteousness" (Gen. 15:5–6).

The word *counted* is a legal or financial term; it means "to put to one's account." As a sinner, Abraham's spiritual bankbook was empty. He was bankrupt! But he trusted God, and God put *righteous* on Abraham's account. Abraham did not work for this righteousness; he received it as a gift from God. He was declared righteous by faith. He was justified by faith (read Rom. 4).

Justification is an important doctrine in the Bible. Justification is the act of God whereby He declares the believing sinner righteous on the basis of Christ's finished work on the cross. It is not a process; it is an act. It is not something the sinner does; it is something God does for the sinner when he trusts Christ. It is a once-for-all event. It never changes.

How can you tell if a person is justified by faith if this transaction takes place between the sinner and God privately? Abraham's example answers that important question: The justified person has a changed life and obeys God's will. His faith is demonstrated by his works.

James used another event in Abraham's life, an event that took place many years after Abraham's conversion. This event is the offering up of Isaac on the altar (Gen. 22). Abraham was not saved by obeying God's difficult command. His obedience proved that he already was saved. "You see that his faith and his actions were working together, and his faith was made complete by what he did" (James 2:22 NIV). There is a perfect relationship between faith and works. As someone has expressed it, "Abraham was not saved by faith plus works, but by a faith that works."

How was Abraham "justified by works" (James 2:21) when he had already been "justified by faith" (see Rom. 4)? By faith, he was justified *before God* and his righteousness declared; by works he was justified *before men* and his righteousness demonstrated. It is true that no humans actually saw Abraham put his son on the altar, but the inspired record in Genesis 22 enables us to see the event and witness Abraham's faith demonstrated by his works.

As I mentioned in the previous chapter, D. L. Moody often said, "Every Bible should be bound in shoe leather." He did not say that because he had been a successful shoe salesman; he said it because he was a dedicated Christian. Dynamic faith obeys God and proves itself in daily life and works. Alas, we still have church members today who fit the description given in Titus: "They profess that they know God; but in works they deny him" (Titus 1:16). Paul also wrote, "This is a faithful saying, and these things I will that thou affirm constantly, that they which have believed in God might be careful to maintain good works" (Titus 3:8).

James' second illustration is Rahab, and the background for her is found in Joshua 2 and 6. Israel was about to invade their Promised Land and take the city of Jericho. Joshua sent spies into the city to get the lay of the land. There they met Rahab, a harlot, who protected them and affirmed that she believed in what God had said and what God was going to do. When the men departed, they promised to save her and her family when the city was taken, and this they did.

It is an exciting story. But in it is one of the Bible's great examples of saving faith (see Heb. 11:31). Rahab heard the Word and knew that her city was condemned. This truth affected her and her fellow citizens so that their hearts melted within them (Josh. 2:11). Rahab responded with her mind and her emotions, but she also responded with her will: *She did something about it.* She risked her own life to protect the Jewish spies, and she further risked her life by sharing the good news of deliverance with the members of her family. The Hebrew word translated "harlot" in Joshua 2 can also have the wider meaning of an "innkeeper." Rahab ran a guest house, so it was normal for the spies to go there. The Greek word "harlot" in James 2:25 definitely means an immoral person. This is also the meaning in Hebrews 11:31. Matthew 1:5 indicates she married into Israel and became an ancestress of our Lord. What grace! Rahab is one of the first soul winners in the Bible, and you cannot help but compare her with the "bad Samaritan" in John 4.

Rahab could have had *dead* faith, a mere intellectual experience. Or she could have had *demonic* faith, her mind enlightened and her emotions stirred. But she exercised *dynamic* faith: Her mind knew the truth, her heart was stirred by the truth, and her will acted on the truth. She proved her faith by her works.

When you realize the small amount of information Rahab had, you can see how truly marvelous her faith really was. Today we have the full revelation of God through His Word and His Son. We live on the other side of Calvary, and we have the Holy Spirit to convict and to teach us the Word. "For unto whomsoever much is given, of him shall be much required" (Luke 12:48). Her faith is an indictment against the unbelief of sinners today.

James 2 emphasizes that the mature Christian practices the truth. He does not merely hold to ancient doctrines; he practices those doctrines in his everyday life. His faith is not the dead faith of the intellectuals or the demonic faith of the fallen spirits. It is the dynamic faith of men like Abraham and women like Rahab, faith that changes a life and goes to work for God.

It is important that each professing Christian examine his own heart and life and make sure that he possesses true saving faith, dynamic faith. "Examine yourselves, whether ye be in the faith; prove your own selves" (2 Cor. 13:5a). Satan is the great deceiver; one of his devices is imitation. If he can convince a person that counterfeit faith is true faith, he has that person in his power.

Here are some questions we can ask ourselves as we examine our hearts:

1. Was there a time when I honestly realized I was a sinner and admitted this to myself and to God?

2. Was there a time when my heart stirred me to flee from the wrath to come? Have I ever seriously been alarmed over my sins?

3. Do I truly understand the gospel, that Christ died for my sins and arose again? Do I understand and confess that I cannot save myself?

4. Did I sincerely repent of my sins and turn from them? Or do I secretly love sin and want to enjoy it?

5. Have I trusted Christ and Christ alone for my salvation? Do I enjoy a living relationship with Him through the Word and in the Spirit?

6. Has there been a change in my life? Do I maintain good works, or are my works occasional and weak? Do I seek to grow in the things of the Lord? Can others tell that I have been with Jesus?

7. Do I have a desire to share Christ with others? Or am I ashamed of Him?

8. Do I enjoy the fellowship of God's people? Is worship a delight to me?

9. Am I ready for the Lord's return? Or will I be ashamed when He comes for me?

To be sure, not every Christian has the same personal experience, and there are degrees of sanctification. But for the most part, the preceding spiritual inventory can assist a person in determining his true standing before God.

"Search me, O God, and know my heart: try me, and know my thoughts: and see if there be any wicked way in me, and lead me in the way everlasting" (Ps. 139:23–24).

QUESTIONS FOR PERSONAL REFLECTION
OR GROUP DISCUSSION

1. How would you describe saving faith?

2. How can you recognize people with dead faith?

3. What illustration did James give that depicts a person with dead faith? How does this make you feel?

4. What is the worst danger of dead faith?

5. In "demonic faith," what has been added to the enlightened intellect of dead faith?

6. What is dynamic faith based upon? What does it involve? What does it lead to?

7. Which two Bible characters does James use to illustrate saving faith? What did they have in common?

8. How can you tell if a person is justified?

9. What set Rahab apart from the other citizens of Jericho?

10. How does Satan try to thwart people from having true saving faith? Why does he do this?

Chapter Seven

THE WORLD'S SMALLEST BUT LARGEST TROUBLEMAKER

(James 3:1–12)

J ames has explained to us two characteristics of the mature Christian: he is patient in trouble (James 1) and he practices the truth (James 2). In this section, he shared the third characteristic of the mature believer: He has power over his tongue.

A pastor friend told me about a member of his church who was a notorious gossip. She would "hang on the phone" most of the day, sharing tidbits with any and all who would listen.

She came to the pastor one day and said, "Pastor, the Lord has convicted me of my sin of gossip. My tongue is getting me and others into trouble."

My friend knew she was not sincere because she had gone through that routine before. Guardedly he asked, "Well, what do you plan to do?"

"I want to put my tongue on the altar," she replied with pious fervor.

Calmly my friend replied, "There isn't an altar big enough," and he left her to think it over.

The Christians that James wrote to were apparently having serious problems with their tongues. James had warned them to be "swift to hear, slow to speak, slow to wrath" (James 1:19). The believer who does not bridle his tongue is not truly religious (James 1:26). We must speak and act as though we were already facing Christ in judgment (James 2:12). When you read passages like James 4:1, 11–12, you get the impression that this assembly must have had some interesting meetings!

The power of speech is one of the greatest powers God has given us. With the tongue, man can praise God, pray, preach the Word, and lead the lost to Christ. What a privilege! But with that same tongue he can tell lies that could ruin a man's reputation or break a person's heart. The ability to speak words is the ability to influence others and accomplish tremendous tasks, and yet we take this ability for granted.

In order to impress on us the importance of controlled speech and the great consequences of our words, James gave us six pictures of the tongue: the bit, the rudder, fire, a poisonous animal, a fountain, and a fig tree. You can put these six pictures into three meaningful classifications that reveal the three powers of the tongue.

1. POWER TO DIRECT: THE BIT AND RUDDER (3:1–4)

Apparently, everybody in the assembly wanted to teach and be a spiritual leader, for James had to warn them: "Not many of you should act as teachers, my brothers" (James 3:1 NIV). Perhaps they were impressed with the authority and prestige of the office and forgot about the tremendous responsibility *and accountability!* Those who teach the Word face the stricter judgment. Teachers must use their tongue to share God's truth, and it is easy to commit sins of the tongue. Furthermore, teachers must practice what they teach; otherwise, their teaching is hypocrisy. Think of the damage that can be done by a teacher who is unprepared, or whose spiritual life is not up to par.

But teachers are not the only ones who are tempted and sin; every Christian must admit that "we all stumble in many ways" (James 3:2 NIV).

And sins of the tongue seem to head the list. The person who is able to discipline his tongue gives evidence that he can control his whole body. He proves that he is a mature (perfect) man.

Was James making a mistake by connecting sins of the tongue with sins committed by "the whole body"? No, because *words* usually lead to *deeds*. During World War II we were accustomed to seeing posters that read LOOSE LIPS SINK SHIPS! But loose lips also wreck lives. A person makes an unguarded statement and suddenly finds himself involved in a fight. His tongue has forced the rest of his body to defend itself.

In selecting the bit and the rudder ("helm" in James 3:4 means "rudder"), James presented two items that are small of themselves, yet exercise great power, just like the tongue. A small bit enables the rider to control the great horse, and a small rudder enables the pilot to steer the huge ship. The tongue is a small member in the body, and yet it has the power to accomplish great things.

Both the bit and the rudder must overcome contrary forces. The bit must overcome the wild nature of the horse, and the rudder must fight the winds and currents that would drive the ship off its course. The human tongue also must overcome contrary forces. We have an old nature that wants to control us and make us sin. There are circumstances around us that would make us say things we ought not to say. Sin on the inside and pressures on the outside are seeking to get control of the tongue.

This means that both the bit and the rudder must be under the control of a strong hand. The expert horseman keeps the mighty power of his steed under control, and the experienced pilot courageously steers the ship through the storm. When Jesus Christ controls the tongue, then we need not fear saying the wrong things—or even saying the right things in a wrong way! "Death and life are in the power of the tongue," warned Solomon (Prov. 18:21). No wonder David prayed, "Set a watch,

O Lord, before my mouth; keep the door of my lips. Incline not my heart to any evil thing" (Ps. 141:3–4). David knew that *the heart* is the key to right speech. "Out of the abundance of the heart the mouth speaketh" (Matt. 12:34). When Jesus Christ is the Lord of the heart, then He is Lord of the lips too.

The bit and rudder have the power to direct, which means *they affect the lives of others.* A runaway horse or a shipwreck could mean injury or death to pedestrians or passengers. The words we speak affect the lives of others. A judge says, "Guilty!" or "Not guilty!" and those words affect the destiny of the prisoner, his family, and his friends. The president of the United States speaks a few words and signs some papers, and the nation is at war. Even a simple yes or no from the lips of a parent can greatly affect the direction of a child's life.

Never underestimate the guidance you give by the words you speak or do not speak. Jesus spoke to a woman at a well, and her life and the lives of her neighbors experienced a miraculous change (John 4). Peter preached at Pentecost and three thousand souls came to salvation through faith in Christ (Acts 2).

On April 21, 1855, Edward Kimball went into a Boston shoe store and led young Dwight L. Moody to Christ. The result: one of history's greatest evangelists, a man whose ministry still continues. The tongue has the power to direct others to the right choices.

It would do us all good to read frequently the book of Proverbs, and to note especially the many references to speech. "A soft answer turneth away wrath: but grievous words stir up anger" (Prov. 15:1). "Lying lips are abomination to the Lord" (Prov. 12:22). "In the multitude of words there wanteth not sin: but he that refraineth his lips is wise" (Prov. 10:19). Yes, the tongue is like a bit and a rudder: It has the power to direct. How important it is that our tongues direct people in the right way!

2. POWER TO DESTROY: THE FIRE AND ANIMAL (3:5–8)

I was visiting the used bookstores along Charing Cross Road in London, and I remarked to a clerk that there were not as many stores as I expected. "There's a reason for that," he replied. "One night during World War II, the incendiary bombs hit and the fires destroyed at least a million books!"

On another occasion, a friend was taking my wife and me on a tour of the beautiful forests in California, and we came to an ugly section that was burned out. Not only was the face of nature scarred, but millions of dollars of valuable timber had been wiped out. "Somebody's lit cigarette," my friend commented as we drove past the blackened earth.

A fire can begin with just a small spark, but it can grow to destroy a city. A fire reportedly started in the O'Leary barn in Chicago at 8:30 p.m., October 8, 1871; and because that fire spread, over 100,000 people were left homeless, 17,500 buildings were destroyed, and 300 people died. It cost the city over $400 million.

Our words can start fires. "Where no wood is, there the fire goeth out: so where there is no talebearer, the strife ceaseth. As coals are to burning coals, and wood to fire; so is a contentious man to kindle strife" (Prov. 26:20–21). In some churches, there are members or officers who cannot control their tongues, and the result is destruction. Let them move out of town or be replaced in office, and a beautiful spirit of harmony and love takes over.

Like a fire, the tongue can "heat things up." David wrote, "I said, I will take heed to my ways, that I sin not with my tongue.… My heart was hot within me, while I was musing the fire burned: then spake I with my tongue" (Ps. 39:1, 3). Have you ever had that experience? Of course you have! A hot head and a hot heart can lead to burning words that later we will regret. David had a temper, and he had to have God's help in controlling it. No wonder Solomon wrote, "He who restrains his word has knowledge, and he who has a cool spirit is a man of understanding" (Prov. 17:27 NASB). "He who is slow to anger has great understanding, but he who is quick-tempered exalts folly" (Prov. 14:29 NASB).

Fire not only starts small and grows, and creates heat; it also defiles. A friend of mine suffered a fire in the basement of his house, and the smoke and fire damage so soiled the upstairs of the house that the family had to move out while the house was redecorated. Fiery words can defile a home, a Sunday school class, a church. The only thing that can wash away that defilement is the blood of Jesus Christ.

Fire burns and hurts, and our words can burn and hurt. One of the sorrows our Lord had to bear when He was here on earth was the way His enemies talked about Him. They called Him a "man gluttonous and a winebibber" (Matt. 11:19) because He graciously accepted invitations to dine with people the Pharisees did not like. When He performed miracles, they said He was in league with Satan. Even when He was dying on the cross, His enemies could not let Him alone but threw vicious taunts into His face.

Fire spreads, and the more fuel you give it, the faster and farther it will spread. The tongue "setteth on fire the course of nature" (James 3:6), or "sets the whole course of his life on fire" (NIV). James suggested that all of life is connected like a wheel, and therefore we cannot keep things from spreading. A person's entire life can be injured or destroyed by the tongue. Time does not correct the sins of the tongue. We may confess our sins of speech, but the fire keeps on spreading.

As it spreads, fire destroys, and the words we speak have the power to destroy. For every word in Hitler's book *Mein Kampf,* 125 lives were lost in World War II. Our own words may not have caused wars or wrecked cities, but they can break hearts and ruin reputations. They can also destroy souls by sending them into eternity without Christ. How important it is for us to let our speech "be always full of grace, seasoned with salt" (Col. 4:6 NIV).

Not only is the tongue like a fire, but it is also like a dangerous animal. It is restless and cannot be ruled (unruly), and it seeks its prey and then pounces and kills. My wife and I once drove through a safari park, admiring the animals as they moved about in their natural habitat. But there were warning signs posted all over the park: DO NOT LEAVE YOUR CAR! DO NOT OPEN YOUR WINDOWS! Those "peaceful animals" were capable of doing great damage, and even killing.

Some animals are poisonous, and some tongues spread poison. The deceptive thing about poison is that it works secretly and slowly, and then kills. How many times has some malicious person injected a bit of poison into the conversation, hoping it would spread and finally get to the person he or she wanted to hurt? As a pastor, I have seen poisonous tongues do great damage to individuals, families, classes, and entire churches. Would you turn hungry lions or angry snakes loose in your Sunday morning service? Of course not! But unruly tongues accomplish the same results.

James reminds us that animals can be tamed, and, for that matter, fire can be tamed. When you tame an animal, you get a worker instead of a destroyer. When you control fire, you generate power. The tongue cannot be tamed by man, but it can be tamed by God. Your tongue need not be "set on fire of hell" (James 3:6). Like the apostles at Pentecost, it can be set on fire from heaven! If God lights the fire and controls it, then the tongue can be a mighty tool for the winning of the lost and the building up of the church. The important thing, of course, is the heart, for it is "out of the abundance of the heart that the mouth speaketh" (Matt. 12:34). If the heart is filled with hatred, Satan will light the fire. But if the heart is filled with love, God will light the fire.

3. POWER TO DELIGHT: THE FOUNTAIN AND TREE (3:9–12)

The fountain, of course, provides the cool water that man needs to stay alive. In underdeveloped countries, the presence of a freshwater fountain is a great blessing to a village. Man needs water not only for drinking, but also for washing, cooking, farming, and a host of other activities so necessary to life.

"The words of a man's mouth are as deep waters, and the wellspring of wisdom as a flowing brook" (Prov. 18:4). "The mouth of a righteous man is a well of life" (Prov. 10:11). "The law of the wise is a fountain of life, to depart from the snares of death" (Prov. 13:14). These verses parallel what James has written and underscore the importance of our words.

Water is life-giving, and our words can give life. However, if water is not controlled, it brings death and destruction. The famous Johnstown, Pennsylvania, flood of 1889 took 2,200 lives and destroyed $10 million in property. "Death and life are in the power of the tongue" (Prov. 18:21).

However, when we bend over a fountain for a drink of cool water, we rarely think of floods. We think only of the precious gift of refreshment that comes with a drink of water. We could not be healthy without water. "There is that speaketh like the piercings of a sword: but the tongue of the wise is health" (Prov. 12:18). Paul's prayer was that he might "refresh" the saints in Rome when he came to them (Rom. 15:32). He often named Christians who had refreshed him (1 Cor. 16:18; Philem. 7, 20).

Water also cleanses. There was a laver in the Old Testament tabernacle and temple that provided for the cleansing of the priests' hands and feet. God's Word is the spiritual water that cleanses us (John 15:3; Eph. 5:26–27). But our words to others can also help to cleanse and sanctify them. Our words ought to be like that river described in Ezekiel 47 that brought life to everything it touched.

The tongue is also delightful because it is like a tree. In Bible lands, trees are vitally important to the economy: They help to hold down the soil; they provide beauty and shade; and they bear fruit. Our words can help to shelter and encourage a weary traveler, and can help to feed a hungry soul. "The lips of the righteous feed many" (Prov. 10:21). Jesus said, "The words that I speak unto you, they are spirit, and they are life" (John 6:63). As we share His Word with others, we feed them and encourage them along the way.

The most important thing about a tree is the root system. If the roots do not go down deep, the tree will not grow in a healthy manner. If we are rooted in the things of the Lord, then our words will be the fruit of our fellowship with Him. We will be like that "blessed man" in Psalm 1 and produce fruit in due season. One reason our Lord was able to say the right words at the right times was because He communed with His Father and heard from heaven each day. Listen to His testimony:

"The Lord God hath given me the tongue of the learned, that I should know how to speak a word in season to him that is weary: he wakeneth morning by morning, he wakeneth mine ear to hear as the learned" (Isa. 50:4). "And in the morning, rising up a great while before day, he went out, and departed into a solitary place, and there prayed" (Mark 1:35).

If you and I are going to have tongues that delight, then we must meet with the Lord each day and learn from Him. We must get our "spiritual roots" deep into His Word. We must pray and meditate and permit the Spirit of God to fill our hearts with God's love and truth.

But James issued a warning: A fountain cannot give forth two kinds of water, and a tree cannot bear two different kinds of fruit. We expect the fountain to flow with sweet water at all times, and we expect the fig tree to bear figs and the olive tree to bear olives. Nature reproduces after its kind.

If the tongue is inconsistent, there is something radically wrong with the heart. I heard about a professing Christian who got angry on the job and let loose with some oaths. Embarrassed, he turned to his partner and said, "I don't know why I said that. It really isn't in me." His partner wisely replied, "It had to be in you or it couldn't have come out of you." When Peter was out of fellowship with Christ, he uttered some oaths, but he went out and wept bitterly and confessed his sins.

The tongue that blesses the Father, and then turns around and curses men made in God's image, is in desperate need of spiritual medicine! How easy it is to sing the hymns during the worship service, then after the service, get into the family car and argue and fight all the way home! "My brethren, these things ought not so to be."

The problem, of course, is not the tongue; it is the heart. It is easy to have "bitter envying and strife" in our hearts (James 3:14). "But those things which proceed out of the mouth come forth from the heart; and they defile the man" (Matt. 15:18). "Keep thy heart with all diligence, for out of it are the issues of life" (Prov. 4:23). As we fill our hearts with God's Word and yield to the Holy Spirit, He can use us to bring delight to others, and we will be refreshing fountains and trees.

As I close this chapter, let me suggest that you start using the "twelve words that can transform your life." If you use these words *and sincerely mean what you say from your heart,* you will find that God will use you to be a blessing and encouragement to others. There are only twelve of them, but they work.

"Please" and **"Thank you."** When you use these three words, you are treating others like people and not things. You are showing appreciation.

"I'm sorry." These two words have a way of breaking down walls and building bridges.

"I love you." Too many people read "romance" into these words, but they go much deeper than that. As Christians, we should love the brethren and even love our enemies. "I love you" is a statement that can carry tremendous power.

"I'm praying for you." And be sure that you are. When you talk to God about people, then you can talk to people about God. Our private praying for people helps us in our public meeting with people. Of course, we never say "I'm praying for you" in a boastful way, as though we are more spiritual than others. We say it in an encouraging way, to let others know that we care enough for them to meet them at the throne of grace.

Yes, the smallest but largest troublemaker in all the world is the tongue. But it does not have to be a troublemaker! God can use our tongues to direct others into the way of life, and to delight them in the trials of life. The tongue is a little member, but it has great power.

Give God your tongue and your heart each day and ask Him to use you to be a blessing to others.

QUESTIONS FOR PERSONAL REFLECTION
OR GROUP DISCUSSION

1. How have you been hurt by someone's words? How have you been helped by someone's words?

2. What are the three powers of the tongue?

3. Why are sins of the tongue connected with sins committed by the whole body?

4. What is the significance of the illustrations of the bit and the rudder?

5. What contrary forces do the bit and rudder (and the tongue) need to overcome?

6. How is the tongue like a fire and like an animal?

7. In what ways can words destroy?

8. When have you seen words bring delight?

9. Why is the tongue compared to a tree?

10. What are the "twelve words that can transform your life"? What words might you add to this list?

Chapter Eight

WHERE TO GET WISDOM

(James 3:13–18)

Wisdom was an important thing to Jewish people. They realized that it was not enough to have knowledge; you had to have wisdom to be able to use that knowledge correctly. All of us know people who are very intelligent, perhaps almost geniuses, and yet who seemingly are unable to carry out the simplest tasks of life. They can program computers but they cannot manage their own lives! "Wisdom is the principal thing; therefore get wisdom" (Prov. 4:7).

James continued to exhort the people in the assembly who wanted to be teachers of the Word (James 3:1). It is not enough simply to stand before the people and say words—*you must have something to say!* This is where spiritual wisdom comes in. Knowledge enables us to take things apart, but wisdom enables us to put things together and relate God's truth to daily life. All of us have heard preachers and teachers who say many good things, but who somehow miss the heart of God's message and fail to relate truth to everyday life. It is this kind of "knowledge without wisdom" that James was writing about. He was contrasting true wisdom and false wisdom in three different aspects.

1. Contrast in Origins (3:15, 17a)

True wisdom comes from above, but false wisdom comes from below. In other words, there is a "heavenly wisdom" that comes from God, and there is a "man-made wisdom" that does not come from God. Whatever does not come from God is destined to fail, no matter how successful it may seem at the time.

The Bible contains many examples of the folly of man's wisdom. The building of the Tower of Babel seemed like a wise enterprise, but it ended in failure and confusion (Gen. 11:1–9). It seemed wise for Abraham to go to Egypt when famine came to Canaan, but the results proved otherwise (Gen. 12:10–20). King Saul thought it was wise to put his own armor on young David for the lad's battle with Goliath, but God's plan was otherwise (1 Sam. 17:38ff.). The disciples thought it was wise to dismiss the great crowd and let them find their own food; but Jesus took a few loaves and fishes and fed the multitude. The Roman "experts" in Acts 27 thought it was wise to leave port and set sail for Rome, even though Paul disagreed, and the storm that followed proved that Paul's wisdom was better than their expert counsel. They lived to regret it, but they lived!

What is the origin of man's wisdom? "This wisdom descendeth not from above, but is earthly, sensual, devilish" (James 3:15). The believer has three enemies: the world, the flesh, and the Devil (Eph. 2:1–3). These enemies are suggested by the terms "earthly, sensual, devilish."

There is a "wisdom of this world" (1 Cor. 1:20–21). Do not confuse the world's *knowledge* and the world's *wisdom*. Certainly, there is a great deal of knowledge in this world, and we all benefit from it, but there is not much wisdom. Man unlocks the secrets of the universe, but he does not know what to do with them. Almost everything he discovers or devises turns against him. Over a century ago, Henry David Thoreau warned that we had "improved means to unimproved ends."

Whenever I ride a bus or elevated train in the city, I often think of the man in Boston who was entertaining a famous Chinese scholar. He met his Asian friend at the train station and rushed him to the subway. As they ran through the subway station, the host panted to his guest, "If we run and catch this next train, we will save three minutes!" To which the patient Chinese philosopher replied, "And what significant thing shall we do with the three minutes we are saving?"

The world by its wisdom knew not God, and in its wisdom rejects the very gospel of God. "For the preaching of the cross is to them that perish foolishness" (1 Cor. 1:18). Any person enamored with the wisdom of this world ought to read the first two chapters of 1 Corinthians and notice how much Paul had to say about God's wisdom and man's wisdom. Man's wisdom is foolishness to God (1 Cor. 1:20), and God's wisdom is foolishness to man (1 Cor. 2:14). Man's wisdom comes from reason, while God's wisdom comes from revelation. Man's worldly wisdom will come to nothing (1 Cor. 1:19), while God's wisdom will endure forever.

Because the world has turned from God, it has lost its wisdom. Every increase in man's knowledge only magnifies the problems. "The fear of the LORD is the beginning of wisdom: and the knowledge of the holy is understanding" (Prov. 9:10). "There is no fear of God before their eyes" (Rom. 3:18).

But this false wisdom has another source: It is "sensual," that is, it is "natural." The Greek word is *psukikos,* which comes from the Greek word *psuke* meaning "life," or "soul." Our English word *psychology* is derived from it. In 1 Corinthians 2:14 and 15:44, 46, *psukikos* is translated "natural," referring to the opposite of "spiritual." In Jude 19 it is translated "sensual." The main idea seems to be that of man's fallen nature as opposed to the new nature given by God. There is a wisdom that gets its origin in man's nature totally apart from the Spirit of God.

But this "wisdom that is from beneath" is also "devilish." Perhaps the best translation is "demonic." Beginning with Genesis 3, where Satan successfully deceived Eve, and continuing through the entire Bible, there is a "wisdom of Satan" at work, fighting against the wisdom of God. Satan convinced Eve that she would be like God. He told her that the tree would make her wise. Ever since that event, people have continued to believe Satan's lies and have tried to become their own gods (Rom. 1:18–25). Satan is cunning; he is the old serpent! He has wisdom that will confound and confuse you if you do not know the wisdom of God.

In contrast to the wisdom that is earthly, sensual, and devilish, James described a "wisdom that is from above" (James 3:17). "Every good gift and every perfect gift is from above" (James 1:17). The Christian looks up to heaven for all that he needs. His citizenship is in heaven (Phil. 3:20), just as his Father is in heaven (Matt. 6:9). His treasures are in heaven, not on earth (Matt. 6:19ff.). He was born from above (John 3:1–7) when he trusted Jesus Christ. The believer's home is in heaven (John 14:1–6) and his hope is in heaven. He sets his affection and attention on things above, not on earthly things (Col. 3:1–4).

What is the Christian's wisdom? Does he look to the philosophies of this world? No! To begin with, Jesus Christ is our wisdom (1 Cor. 1:24, 30). In Jesus Christ "are hid all the treasures of wisdom and knowledge" (Col. 2:3). The first step toward true wisdom is the receiving of Jesus Christ as Savior.

The Word of God is also our wisdom. "Behold, I have taught you statutes and judgments.… Keep therefore and do them; for this is your wisdom and your understanding in the sight of the nations" (Deut. 4:5–6). The Scriptures are able to make us "wise unto salvation" (2 Tim. 3:15).

James 1:5 indicates that we find wisdom through believing prayer. "If any of you lack wisdom, let him ask of God." The Holy Spirit of God is "the

Spirit of wisdom and revelation" (Eph. 1:17), and He directs us in the wisest paths as we trust the Word and pray.

The origin of true spiritual wisdom is God. To get your wisdom from any other source is to ask for trouble. There is no need to get the counterfeit wisdom of the world, the wisdom that caters to the flesh and accomplishes the work of the Devil. Get your wisdom from God!

2. Contrast in Operations (3:13–14, 17)

The wisdom from above, God's wisdom, operates in a different way from the wisdom that is "earthly, sensual, devilish." Since they originate from radically different sources, they must operate in opposite ways.

What are the evidences of false wisdom?

Envy (v. 14a). This word carries the meaning of selfish ambition and zeal. It ties in with James 3:1, where James warned them not to be ambitious for spiritual offices. The wisdom of the world says, "Promote yourself. You're as good as the other candidates, maybe better! The wheel that squeaks the loudest gets the grease." Sad to say, there is a great deal of selfish, carnal promotion among God's people. Even the apostles argued over who was the greatest in the kingdom.

It is easy to go on an ego trip under the guise of spiritual zeal. The Pharisees used their religious activities to promote the praise of men (Matt. 6:1–18). We ought to be zealous in the things of the Lord, but we must be sure that our motives are right. The wisdom of this world exalts man and robs God of glory. In 1 Corinthians 1:17ff., Paul discussed the wisdom of God and the wisdom of this world, and he explained why God works as He does: "That no flesh should glory in his presence" (1 Cor. 1:29). He concluded the section with the admonition, "He that glorieth, let him glory in the Lord" (1 Cor. 1:31).

Is our zeal for the Lord spiritual or carnal? Do we rejoice when others succeed, or do we have secret envy and criticism? Do we feel burdened when others fail, or are we glad? When the wisdom of the world gets into the church, there is a great deal of fleshly promotion and human glorification. Beware!

Strife (v. 14b). This word means "party spirit." It was used by the Greeks to describe a politician out canvassing for votes. The world's wisdom says, "Get all the support you can! Ask the people in the church if they are for you or against you!" Of course, this spirit of self-seeking only creates rivalry and division in the church. "Let nothing be done through strife or vainglory; but in lowliness of mind let each esteem other better than [more important than] themselves" (Phil. 2:3).

Boasting (v. 14c). Pride loves to boast, and nothing is prouder than the wisdom of men. There is a way to report blessings so that God gets the glory, but there is also an approach that gives men the praise. It is tragic to see mutual admiration societies among God's people. In 2 Corinthians 10, when Paul was forced to boast about his ministry, he was careful to give God the glory. "Of course we shouldn't dare include ourselves in the same class as those who write their own testimonials, or even to compare ourselves with them! All they are doing, of course, is to measure themselves by their own standards or by comparisons within their own circle, and that doesn't make for accurate estimation, you may be sure" (2 Cor. 10:12 PH).

When God's wisdom is at work, there is a sense of humility and submission, and you want God to get all the glory. You have no desire to compare yourself with any other Christian, because you see only Christ—and compared with Him, all of us still have a long way to go!

Deceit (v. 14d). "Lie not against the truth." The sequence is not difficult to understand. First, there is selfish ambition that leads to party spirit and rivalry. In order to "win the election" we must resort to boasting; *and boasting usually involves lies!* A man's life is not read in his press releases; it is read by the Lord in his heart. "Therefore judge nothing before the time, until the Lord come, who both will bring to light the hidden things of darkness, and will make manifest the counsels of the hearts: and then shall every man have praise of God" (1 Cor. 4:5).

What a relief it is to turn to the evidences of true spiritual wisdom.

Meekness (v. 13). Meekness is not weakness; it is power under control. The meek person does not selfishly assert himself. The Greek word was used for a horse that had been broken so that its power was under control. The meek person seeks only the glory of God and does not cater to the praises of men. Meekness is a fruit of the Spirit (Gal. 5:23); it cannot be manufactured by man. There is a false humility that some people mistake for meekness, but it is only counterfeit.

The phrase "meekness of wisdom" is an interesting one (James 3:3). Meekness is the right use of power, and wisdom is the right use of knowledge. They go together. The truly wise person will show in his daily life (*conversation* means "behavior") that he is a child of God. Attitude and action go together.

Purity (v. 17a). "First pure" indicates the importance of holiness. God is holy; therefore the wisdom from above is pure. The idea behind this word is "chaste, free from defilement." James used it again in James 4:8—"purify your hearts," or, "make chaste your hearts." God's wisdom leads to purity of life. Man's wisdom may lead to sin. There is a spiritual purity that results in a chaste relationship with the Lord (2 Cor. 11:3), and there is a worldliness that makes the person a spiritual adulterer (James 4:4).

Peace (v. 17b). Man's wisdom leads to competition, rivalry, and war (James 4:1–2); but God's wisdom leads to peace. It is a peace based on holiness, not on compromise. God never has "peace at any price." The peace of the church is not more important than the purity of the church. If the church is pure, devoted to God, then there will be peace. "And the work of righteousness shall be peace, and the effect of righteousness quietness and assurance for ever" (Isa. 32:17). The church can never have peace by sweeping sins under the rug and pretending they are not there. Man's wisdom says, "Cover up sin! Keep things together!" God's wisdom says, "Confess sin and My peace will keep things together!"

Gentleness (v. 17c). Matthew Arnold liked to call this "sweet reasonableness." It carries the meaning of moderation without compromise, gentleness without weakness. The gentle person does not deliberately cause fights, but neither does he compromise the truth in order to keep peace. Carl Sandburg described Abraham Lincoln as a man of "velvet steel." That is a good description of gentleness.

Compliance (v. 17d). *God's* wisdom makes the believer agreeable and easy to live with and work with. *Man's* wisdom makes a person hard and stubborn. The compliant person is willing to hear all sides of a question, but he does not compromise his own convictions. He can disagree without being disagreeable. He is "swift to hear, slow to speak, slow to wrath" (James 1:19). Many people think that stubbornness is conviction, and they must have their own way. When God's wisdom is at work, there is a willingness to listen, think, pray, and obey whatever God reveals. "Yielding to persuasion" is another translation of this word.

Mercy (v. 17e). To be "full" of something means to be "controlled by." The person who follows God's wisdom is controlled by mercy. "Be ye therefore merciful, as your Father also is merciful" (Luke 6:36). God in His grace gives us what we do not deserve, and in His mercy He does not give us what we do deserve. Our Lord's parable of the good Samaritan illustrates the meaning of mercy (Luke 10:25–37). For a Samaritan to care for a Jewish stranger was an act of mercy. He could gain nothing from it, except the blessing that comes from doing the will of God, and the victim could not pay him back. That is mercy.

Good fruits (v. 17f). People who are faithful are fruitful. God's wisdom does not make a life empty; it makes it full. The Spirit produces fruit to the glory of God (see John 15:1–16). The lawyer in Luke 10:25–37 was willing to *discuss* the subject of neighborliness, but he was unwilling to be a neighbor and help someone else. God's wisdom is practical; it changes the life and produces good works to the glory of God.

Decisiveness (v. 17g). The word suggests singleness of mind and is the opposite of "wavering" (James 1:6). When you lean on the world's wisdom, you are pressured from one side and then another to change your mind or take a new viewpoint. When you have God's wisdom, you need not waver; you can be decisive and not be afraid. Wisdom from above brings strength from above.

Sincerity (v. 17h). The Greek word translated "hypocrite" in our New Testament means "one who wears a mask, an actor." When man's wisdom is at work, there may be insincerity and pretense. When God's wisdom is at work, there is openness and honesty, "speaking the truth in love" (Eph. 4:15). Wherever you find God's people pretending and hiding, you can be sure the wisdom of this world is governing their ministry. "Religious politics" is an abomination to God. Faith is living without scheming.

There is quite a contrast between the operation of God's wisdom and the operation of the wisdom of this world. It would be profitable for church officers and leaders to evaluate their own lives and their ministries in the light of what James has written. While the local church is an organization, it cannot depend on the "Madison Avenue" methods that make secular businesses succeed. God's ways and God's thoughts are far above us! "Now we have received, not the spirit of the world, but the Spirit which is of God; that we might know the things that are freely given to us of God" (1 Cor. 2:12).

3. CONTRAST IN OUTCOMES (3:16, 18)

Origin determines outcome. Worldly wisdom will produce worldly results; spiritual wisdom will give spiritual results.

Worldly wisdom produces trouble (v. 16): envy, strife, confusion, evil works. It does not appear that God was at work in that assembly. In James 4, James would deal with the "wars and fightings" among the believers. Wrong thinking produces wrong living. One reason the world is in such a mess is because men have refused to accept the wisdom of God.

The word translated "confusion" means "disorder that comes from instability." It is related to "unstable" in James 1:8 and "unruly" in James 3:8. Read 2 Corinthians 12:20 and you will get a description of a church that is confused. Jesus used this word to describe the convulsions of the world in the last days (Luke 21:9).

Jealousy, competition, party spirit—all of these contribute to confusion. The Tower of Babel in Genesis 11 is a good illustration of this fact. From man's point of view, the building of the tower was a wise thing, but from God's viewpoint, the project was stupid and sinful. The result? Confusion. Even today, we use the word *babel* to mean "confusion."

Confusion sets the stage for "every evil work" (James 3:16). *Evil* here means "worthless, of no account." It reminds us of the "wood, hay, stubble" of 1 Corinthians 3:12. A ministry operating in the wisdom of this world may appear to be great and successful, but in the day of judgment it may burn up. "Therefore judge nothing before the time" (1 Cor. 4:5). The church at Smyrna thought it was poor, but the Lord said it was rich; while the "rich church" at Laodicea was declared to be poor (Rev. 2:9; 3:14–22).

The most important thing we can do in our local churches is measure our ministries by the Word of God, not by the wisdom of men. The many battles among Christians, the church splits, the absence of purity and peace, all suggest that something is wrong. Perhaps that "something" is the absence of the wisdom of God.

God's wisdom produces blessing (v. 18). James returned to that word *fruit*. There is a vast difference between man-made results and God-given fruit. Fruit is the product of life, and fruit has in it *the seeds for more fruit*. Usually it is the *seed* that is sown, but here it is the *fruit* that is sown. As we share the fruit of God with others, they are fed and satisfied, and they in turn bear fruit.

The Christian life is a life of sowing and reaping. For that matter, *every* life is a life of sowing and reaping, and we reap just what we sow. The Christian who obeys God's wisdom sows righteousness, not sin; he sows peace, not war. The life we live enables the Lord to bring righteousness and peace into the lives of others.

What we are is what we live, and what we live is what we sow. What we sow determines what we reap. If we live in God's wisdom, we sow righteousness and peace, and we reap God's blessing. If we live in man's worldly wisdom, we sow sin and war, and we reap "confusion and every evil work."

It is a serious thing to be a troublemaker in God's family. One of the sins that God hates is that of sowing "discord among brethren" (read Prov. 6:16–19). Lot followed the world's wisdom and brought trouble to the camp of Abraham; but Abraham followed God's wisdom and brought peace. Lot's decision led to "good-for-nothing works," and everything he lived for went up in smoke at the destruction of Sodom and Gomorrah. Abraham's decision, in the wisdom of God, led to blessings for his own household and ultimately for the whole world (read Gen. 13).

"Happy is the man that findeth wisdom, and the man that getteth understanding" (Prov. 3:13).

QUESTIONS FOR PERSONAL REFLECTION
OR GROUP DISCUSSION

1. In what three aspects does James contrast true wisdom and false wisdom?

2. What are some biblical examples of the folly of man's wisdom?

3. What is the difference between the world's knowledge and the world's wisdom?

4. How can you tell when God's wisdom is at work?

5. In James 3:13–18, what are the evidences of false wisdom? What are the evidences of true wisdom?

6. Which of the evidences of worldly wisdom would you like to see less of in your life?

7. Which of the evidences of wisdom from above would you like to see more of in your life?

8. What results does worldly wisdom produce? What does godly wisdom produce?

9. What is the most important way to measure which wisdom is prevailing in ourselves, our ministries, and our churches?

10. In what way is the Christian life a life of sowing and reaping?

Chapter Nine

How to End Wars

(James 4:1–12)

H ave you ever heard of the "War of the Whiskers" or the "War of the Oaken Bucket"? How about the "War of Jenkins' Ear"? These were actual wars fought between nations, and you can read about them in most history books.

War is a fact of life, in spite of treaties, world peace organizations, and the threat of atomic bombs. Not only are there wars between nations, but there are wars of one kind or another on almost every level of life—even "gas wars" among filling station operators!

James discussed this important theme of war in this paragraph, and he explained that there are three wars going on in the world. He also told how these wars could be stopped.

1. AT WAR WITH EACH OTHER (4:1A, 11–12)

"What causes fights and quarrels among you?" (NIV). Among Christians! "Behold, how good and how pleasant it is for brethren to dwell together in unity" (Ps. 133:1). Surely *brethren* should live together in love and harmony, yet often they do not. Lot caused a quarrel with his uncle Abraham (Gen. 13). Absalom created a war for his father David (2 Sam. 13—18). Even the disciples created problems for the Lord when they argued over who was the greatest in the kingdom (Luke 9:46–48).

When you examine some of the early churches, you discover that they had their share of disagreements. The members of the Corinthian church were competing with each other in the public meetings, and even suing each other in court (1 Cor. 6:1–8; 14:23–40). The Galatian believers were "biting and devouring" one another (Gal. 5:15). Paul had to admonish the Ephesians to cultivate spiritual unity (Eph. 4:1–16), and even his beloved church at Philippi had problems: Two women could not get along with each other (Phil. 4:1–3).

James mentioned several different kinds of disagreements among the saints.

Class wars (2:1–9). Here is that age-old rivalry between the rich and the poor. The rich man gets the attention, the poor man is ignored. The rich man is honored, the poor man is disgraced. How tragic it is when local churches get their values confused and cater to the rich, while they ignore, or even reject, the poor. If fellowship in a church depends on such external things as clothing and economic status, then the church is out of the will of God.

Employment wars (5:1–6). Again, it is the rich man who has the power to control and hurt the poor man. Laborers do not get their wages, or they do not get their fair wages. In spite of our modern labor movement and federal legislation, there are still many people who cannot get a good job, or whose income is less than adequate for the work they are doing.

Church fights (1:19–20; 3:13–18). Apparently, the believers James wrote to were at war with each other over positions in the church, many of them wanting to be teachers and leaders. When they studied the Word, the result was not edification, but strife and arguments. Each person thought that his ideas were the only right ideas and his ways the only right ways. Self-ish ambition ruled their meetings, not spiritual submission.

Personal wars (4:11–12). The saints were speaking evil of one another and judging one another. Here, again, we see the wrong use of the tongue. Christians are to speak "the truth in love" (Eph. 4:15); they are not to speak evil in a spirit of rivalry and criticism. If the truth about a brother is harmful, then we should cover it in love and not repeat it (1 Peter 4:8). If he has sinned, we should go to him personally and try to win him back (Matt. 18:15–19; Gal. 6:1–2).

James was not forbidding us to use discrimination or even to evaluate people. Christians need to have discernment (Phil. 1:9–10), but they must not act like God in passing judgment. We must first examine our own lives, and then try to help others (Matt. 7:1–5). We never know all the facts in a case, and we certainly never know the motives that are at work in men's hearts. To speak evil of a brother and to judge a brother on the basis of partial evidence and (probably) unkind motives is to sin against him and against God. We are not called to be judges; God is the only Judge. He is patient and understanding; His judgments are just and holy; we can leave the matter with Him.

It is unfortunate that the saints are at war with each other, leader against leader, church against church, fellowship against fellowship. The world watches these religious wars and says, "Behold, how they hate one another!" No wonder Jesus prayed, "That they all may be one; as thou, Father, art in me, and I in thee, that they also may be one in us: that the world may believe that thou hast sent me" (John 17:21).

But, why are we at war with one another? We belong to the same family; we trust the same Savior; we are indwelt by the same Holy Spirit—and yet we fight one another. Why? James answered this question by explaining the second war that is going on.

2. AT WAR WITH OURSELVES (4:1B–3)

"What causes fights and quarrels among you? Don't they come from your desires that battle within you?" (James 4:1 NIV). The war in the heart is helping to cause the wars in the church! "But if ye have bitter envying and strife in your hearts, glory not, and lie not against the truth.... For where envying and strife is, there is confusion and every evil work" (James 3:14, 16).

The essence of sin is selfishness. Eve disobeyed God because she wanted to eat of the tree and become wise like God. Abraham lied about his wife because he selfishly wanted to save his own life (Gen. 12:10–20). Achan caused defeat to Israel because he selfishly took some forbidden loot from the ruins of Jericho (Josh. 7). "We have turned every one to his own way" (Isa. 53:6).

Often we veil our religious quarrels under the disguise of "spirituality." We are like Miriam and Aaron, who complained about Moses' wife, but who really were envious of Moses' authority (Num. 12). Or we imitate James and John, who asked for special thrones in the kingdom, when what they really wanted was recognition today (Mark 10:35–45). In both of these instances, the result of selfish desire was chastening and division among God's people. Miriam's sin halted the progress of Israel for a whole week!

Selfish desires are dangerous things. They lead to *wrong actions* ("ye kill, ... ye fight and war," James 4:2), and they even lead to *wrong praying* ("When you ask, you do not receive, because you ask with wrong motives, that you may spend what you get on your pleasures," James 4:3 NIV). When our praying is wrong, our whole Christian life is wrong. It has well been said that the purpose of prayer is not to get man's will done in heaven, but to get God's will done on earth.

"Thou shalt not covet" is the last of God's Ten Commandments, but its violation can make us break all of the other nine! Covetousness can make a person murder, tell lies, dishonor his parents, commit adultery, and in one way or another violate all of God's moral law. Selfish living and selfish praying always lead to war. If there is war on the inside, there will ultimately be war on the outside.

People who are at war with themselves because of selfish desires are always unhappy people. They never enjoy life. Instead of being thankful for the blessings they do have, they complain about the blessings they do not have. They cannot get along with other people because they are always envying others for what they have and do. They are always looking for that "magic something" that will change their lives, when the real problem is within their own hearts.

Sometimes we use prayer as a cloak to hide our true desires. "But I prayed about it!" can be one of the biggest excuses a Christian can use. Instead of seeking God's will, we tell God what He is supposed to do, and we get angry at Him if He does not obey. This anger at God eventually spills over and we get angry at God's people. More than one church split has been caused by saints who take out their frustrations with God on the members of the church. Many a church or family problem would be solved if people would only look into their own hearts and see the battles raging there.

God made us a unity; mind, emotions, and will should work together. James stated the reason we are at war with ourselves and, consequently, with each other.

3. AT WAR WITH GOD (4:4–10)

The root cause of every war, internal and external, is rebellion against God. At the beginning of creation, you behold perfect harmony, but sin came into the world, and this led to conflict. Sin is lawlessness (1 John 3:4), and lawlessness is rebellion against God.

How does a believer declare war against God? By being friendly with God's enemies. James named three enemies that we must not fraternize with if we want to be at peace with God.

(1) The world (v. 4). By the "world," James means, of course, human society apart from God. The whole system of things in this society of ours is anti-Christ and anti-God. Abraham was the friend of God (James 2:23); Lot was the friend of the world. Lot ended up in a war, and Abraham had to rescue him (Gen. 14).

A Christian gets involved with the world *gradually*, as I pointed out in chapter 4 of this study. First, there is "the friendship of the world" (James 4:4). This results in being "spotted" by the world (James 1:27) so that areas of our lives meet with the approval of the world. Friendship leads to loving the world (1 John 2:15–17), and this makes it easy to conform to the world (Rom. 12:2). The sad result is being condemned with the world (1 Cor. 11:32), our souls saved "yet as by fire" (1 Cor. 3:11–15).

Friendship with the world is compared to adultery. The believer is "married to Christ" (Rom. 7:4) and ought to be faithful to Him. The Jewish Christians who read this letter would understand this picture of "spiritual adultery" because the prophets Ezekiel, Jeremiah, and Hosea used it when rebuking Judah for her sins (see Jer. 3:1–5; Ezek. 23; Hos. 1—2). By adopting the sinful ways of the other nations, and by worshipping their gods, the nation of Judah committed adultery against her God.

The world is the enemy of God, and whoever wills to be a friend of the world cannot be the friend of God. Neither can he be if he lives for the flesh, for this is the second enemy James named.

(2) The flesh (vv. 1, 5). By "the flesh" is meant the old nature that we inherited from Adam, that is prone to sin. The flesh is not the body. The body is not sinful; the body is neutral. The Spirit may use the body to glorify God, or the flesh may use the body to serve sin. When a sinner yields to Christ, he receives a new nature within, but the old nature is neither removed nor reformed. For this reason, there is a battle within: "For the sinful nature desires what is contrary to the Spirit, and the Spirit what is contrary to the sinful nature. They are in conflict with each other, so that you do not do what you want" (Gal. 5:17 NIV). This is what James termed "your lusts that are in your members" (James 4:1).

Living for the flesh means grieving the Holy Spirit of God who lives in us. "Or do you think Scripture says without reason that the Spirit he caused to live in us longs jealously?" (James 4:5 NIV, margin). Just as the world is the enemy of God the Father, so the flesh is the enemy of God the Holy Spirit. There is a holy, loving jealousy that a husband and wife have over each other, and rightly so. The Spirit within jealously guards our relationship to God, and the Spirit is grieved when we sin against God's love.

Living to please the old nature means to declare war against God. "The carnal mind is enmity against God" (Rom. 8:7). To allow the flesh to control the mind is to lose the blessing of fellowship with God. Abraham had a spiritual mind; he walked with God and enjoyed peace. Lot had a carnal mind; he disobeyed God and experienced war. "For to be carnally minded is death; but to be spiritually minded is life and peace" (Rom. 8:6).

(3) The Devil (vv. 6–7). The world is in conflict with the Father; the flesh fights against the Holy Spirit; and the Devil opposes the Son of God. Pride is Satan's great sin, and it is one of his chief weapons in his warfare against the saint and the Savior. God wants us to be humble; Satan wants us to be proud. "You will be like God," Satan promised Eve, and she believed him. A new Christian must not be put into places of spiritual leadership "lest being lifted up with pride he fall into the condemnation of the devil" (1 Tim. 3:6).

God wants us to depend on His grace ("But he giveth more grace"), while the Devil wants us to depend on ourselves. Satan is the author of all "do-it-yourself" spiritual enterprises. He enjoys inflating the ego and encouraging the believer to do it his own way. In spite of Jesus' warnings about Satan's plans, Peter fell into the snare, pulled out his sword, and tried to accomplish God's will in his own way. What a mess he made of things!

One of the problems in our churches today is that we have too many celebrities and not enough servants. Christian workers are promoted so much that there is very little place left for God's glory. Man has nothing to be proud of in himself. There dwells no good thing in us (Rom. 7:18), but when we trust Christ, He puts that "good thing" in us that makes us His children (2 Tim. 1:6, 14).

Here, then, are three enemies that want to turn us away from God: the world, the flesh, and the Devil. These enemies are left over from our old life of sin (Eph. 2:1–3). Christ has delivered us from them, but they still attack us. How can we overcome them? How can we be the friends of God and the enemies of the world, the flesh, and the Devil? James gave us three instructions to follow if we would enjoy peace instead of war.

(1) Submit to God (v. 7). This word is a military term that means "get into your proper rank." When a buck private acts like the general, there is going to be trouble! Unconditional surrender is the only way to complete victory. If there is any area of the life kept back from God, there will always be battles. This explains why uncommitted Christians cannot live with themselves or with other people.

"Neither give place to the devil," cautioned Paul in Ephesians 4:27. Satan needs a foothold in our lives if he is going to fight against God, and *we give him that foothold*. The way to resist the Devil is to submit to God.

After King David committed adultery with Bathsheba and killed her husband, he hid his sins for almost a year. There was war between him and God, and David had declared it. Read Psalms 32 and 51 to discover the high price David paid to be at war with God. When he finally submitted to God, David experienced peace and joy. This too he recorded in Psalms 32 and 51. Submission is an act of the will; it is saying, "Not my will but thine be done."

(2) Draw near to God (v. 8). How do we do this? By confessing our sins and asking for His cleansing. "Cleanse your hands, ye sinners; and purify your hearts, ye double-minded." The Greek word translated "purify" means "make chaste." This parallels the idea of "spiritual adultery" in James 4:4.

Dr. A. W. Tozer has a profound essay in one of his books, titled "Nearness Is Likeness." He says the more we are like God, the nearer we are to God. I may be sitting in my living room with my Siamese cat on my lap, and my wife may be twenty feet away in the kitchen, yet I am nearer to my wife than to the cat because the cat is unlike me. We have very little in common.

God graciously draws near to us when we deal with the sin in our lives that keeps Him at a distance. He will not share us with anyone else; He must have complete control. The double-minded Christian can never be close to God. Again, Abraham and Lot come to mind. Abraham "drew near" and talked to God about Sodom (Gen. 18:23ff.), while Lot moved into Sodom and lost the blessing of God.

(3) Humble yourselves before God (vv. 9–10). It is possible to submit outwardly and yet not be humbled inwardly. God hates the sin of pride (Prov. 6:16–17), and He will chasten the proud believer until he is humbled. We have a tendency to treat sin too lightly, even to laugh about it ("let your laughter be turned into mourning"). But sin is serious, and one mark of true humility is facing the seriousness of sin and dealing with our disobedience. "A broken and a contrite heart, O God, thou wilt not despise" (Ps. 51:17).

Sometimes we hear a believer pray, "O Lord, humble me!" That is a dangerous thing to pray. Far better that we humble ourselves before God, confess our sins, weep over them, and turn from them. "To this man will I look, even to him that is poor and of a contrite spirit, and trembleth at my word" (Isa. 66:2). "The LORD is nigh unto them that are of a broken heart; and saveth such as be of a contrite spirit" (Ps. 34:18).

If we obey these three instructions, then God will draw near, cleanse us, and forgive us; *and the wars will cease!* We will not be at war with God, so we will not be at war with ourselves. This means we will not be at war with others. "And the work of righteousness shall be peace; and the effect of righteousness quietness and assurance forever" (Isa. 32:17).

Put the government of your life on His shoulders, and let Him become the Prince of Peace in your life (Isa. 9:6).

QUESTIONS FOR PERSONAL REFLECTION
OR GROUP DISCUSSION

1. What were some of the disagreements causing Christians to war with each other in James' day?

2. What are some of the reasons Christians war against each other today?

3. Why are these wars a particularly sad commentary on Christians today? (See John 13:34–35.)

4. What is the difference between the kind of judging encouraged in Matthew 7:15–20 and the kind of judging discouraged in James 4:11–12 and Matthew 7:1–5?

5. Why does Wiersbe say that the essence of sin is selfishness? How can you relate to this personally?

6. How is it possible to "spiritually" rationalize our quarrels with other Christians?

7. How can a Christian pray wrongly?

8. Why do you think Wiersbe states that the first two wars (with each other and with ourselves) are really caused by a third war—a war against God? How do people declare war against God?

9. Why do you think it is often easy for the Christian to be drawn into friendship with the world?

10. In James 4:6, what is the relationship between grace and pride?

Chapter Ten

PLAN AHEAD

(James 4:13–17)

James began chapter 4 talking about war with God, and he ended it talking about the will of God. But the two themes are related: When a believer is out of the will of God, he becomes a troublemaker and not a peacemaker.

Lot moved into Sodom and brought trouble to his family. David committed adultery and brought trouble to his family and his kingdom. Jonah disobeyed God and almost sent a shipload of heathen sailors into a watery grave. In each case, there was a wrong attitude toward the will of God.

That God would have a plan for each of our lives is an obvious truth. He is a God of *wisdom* and knows what ought to happen and when it should occur. And, as a God of *love*, He must desire the very best for His children. Too many Christians look on the will of God as bitter medicine they must take, instead of seeing it as the gracious evidence of the love of God.

"I would give my life to the Lord, but I'm afraid," a perplexed teenager told me at a church youth conference.

"What are you afraid of?" I asked.

"I'm afraid God will ask me to do something dangerous!"

"The dangerous life is not *in* the will of God," I replied, "but *out* of the will of God. The safest place in the world is right where God wants you."

I was going through a difficult time in my own ministry some years ago, questioning the will of God. While on vacation, I was reading the book of Psalms, asking God to give me some assurance and encouragement. Psalm 33:11 was the answer to that prayer: "The counsel of the LORD standeth for ever, the thoughts of his heart to all generations."

"The *will* of God comes from the *heart* of God," I said to myself. "His will is the expression of His love, so I don't have to be afraid!" It was a turning point in my life to discover the blessing of loving and living the will of God.

In this section of his letter, James pointed out three attitudes toward the will of God. Of course, only one of them is the correct one, the one that every Christian ought to cultivate.

1. IGNORING GOD'S WILL (4:13–14, 16)

Perhaps James was addressing the wealthy merchants in the assembly. They might have discussed their business deals and boasted about their plans. There is no evidence that they sought the will of God or prayed about their decisions. They measured success in life by how many times they got their own way and accomplished what they had planned.

But James presented four arguments that revealed the foolishness of ignoring the will of God.

(1) The complexity of life (v. 13). Think of all that is involved in life: today, tomorrow, buying, selling, getting gain, losing, going here, going there. Life is made up of people and places, activities and goals, days and years, and each of us must make many crucial decisions day after day.

Apart from the will of God, life is a mystery. When you know Jesus Christ as your Savior and seek to do His will, then life starts to make sense. Even the physical world around you takes on new meaning. There is a simplicity and unity to your life that makes for poise and confidence. You are no longer living in a mysterious, threatening universe. You can sing, "This is my Father's world!"

(2) The uncertainty of life (v. 14a). This statement is based on Proverbs 27:1—"Boast not thyself of tomorrow; for thou knowest not what a day may bring forth." These businessmen were making plans for a whole year when they could not even see ahead into *one day!* See how confident they were: "We will go. We will stay a year. We will buy and sell and make a profit."

Their attitude reminds us of the farmer in the parable of Jesus in Luke 12:16–21. The man had a bumper crop; his barns were too small; so he decided to build bigger barns and have greater security for the future. "And I will say to my soul, Soul, thou hast much goods laid up for many years; take thine ease, eat, drink, and be merry" (Luke 12:19).

What was God's reply to this man's boasting? "Thou fool, this night thy soul shall be required of thee" (Luke 12:20). Life is not uncertain to God, but it is uncertain to us. Only when we are in His will can we be confident of tomorrow, for we know that He is leading us.

(3) The brevity of life (v. 14b). This is one of the repeated themes of Scripture. To us, life seems long and we measure it in years, but in comparison to eternity, life is but a vapor. James borrowed that figure from the book of Job where you find many pictures of the brevity of life.

"My days are swifter than a weaver's shuttle" (Job 7:6). "The cloud is consumed and vanisheth away" (Job 7:9). "Our days upon earth are a shadow" (Job 8:9). "Now my days are swifter than a post" (Job 9:25), referring to the royal couriers that hastened in their missions. "They are passed away as the swift ships: as the eagle that hasteth to the prey" (Job 9:26). "Man that is born of a woman is of few days and full of trouble. He cometh forth like a flower, and is cut down: he fleeth also as a shadow, and continueth not" (Job 14:1–2).

We count our *years* at each birthday, but God tells us to number our *days* (Ps. 90:12). After all, we live a day at a time, and those days rush by more quickly the older we grow.

Since life is so brief, we cannot afford merely to "spend our lives," and we certainly do not want to "waste our lives." We must *invest our lives* in those things that are eternal.

God reveals His will in His Word, and yet most people ignore the Bible. In the Bible, God gives precepts, principles, and promises that can guide us in every area of life. Knowing and obeying the Word of God is the surest way to success (Josh. 1:8; Ps. 1:3).

(4) The frailty of man (v. 16). "As it is, you boast and brag. All such boasting is evil" (NIV). Man's boasting only covers up man's weakness. "Man proposes but God disposes," wrote Thomas à Kempis. Solomon said it first: "The lot is cast into the lap; but the whole disposing thereof is of the LORD" (Prov. 16:33). Man cannot control future events. He has neither the wisdom to *see* the future nor the power to *control* the future. For him to boast is sin; it is making himself God.

How foolish it is for people to ignore the will of God. It is like going through the dark jungles without a map, or over the stormy seas without a compass. When we visited Mammoth Cave in Kentucky, I was impressed with the maze of tunnels and the dense darkness when the lights were turned off. When we got to the "Pulpit Rock," the man in charge of the tour gave a five-word sermon from it: "Stay close to your guide." Good counsel indeed!

2. DISOBEYING GOD'S WILL (4:17)

These people *know* the will of God but choose to disobey it. This attitude expresses even more pride than does the first; for the person says to God, "I know what You want me to do, but I prefer not to do it. I really know more about this than You do!" "For it had been better for them not to have known the way of righteousness, than, after they have known it, to turn from the holy commandment delivered unto them" (2 Peter 2:21).

Why do people who know the will of God deliberately disobey it? I have already suggested one reason: pride. Man likes to boast that he is the "master of his fate, the captain of his soul." Man has accomplished so many marvelous things that he thinks he can do anything.

Another reason is man's ignorance of the nature of God's will. He acts as though the will of God is something he can accept or reject. In reality, the will of God is not an option; it is an obligation. We cannot "take it or leave it." Because He is the Creator and we are the creatures, we must obey Him. Because He is the Savior and Lord, and we are His children and servants, we must obey Him. To treat the will of God lightly is to invite the chastening of God in our lives.

Many people have the mistaken idea that the will of God is a formula for misery. Just the opposite is true! It is *disobeying* the Lord's will that leads to misery. The Bible and human experience are both witnesses to this truth. And even if a disobedient Christian seems to escape difficulty in this life, what will he say when he faces the Lord? "And that servant, which knew his lord's will, and prepared not himself, neither did according to his will, shall be beaten with many stripes. But he that knew not, and did commit things worthy of stripes, shall be beaten with few stripes" (Luke 12:47–48).

What happens to Christians who deliberately disobey the known will of God? They are chastened by their loving Father until they submit (Heb. 12:5–11). If a professed believer is not chastened, it is evidence that he has never truly been born again but is a counterfeit. God's chastening is an evidence of His love, not His hatred. Just as we earthly fathers spank our children to help them respect our will and obey, so our heavenly Father chastens His own. Though chastening is hard to take, it has a comforting truth of sonship with it.

But there is also the danger of losing heavenly rewards. In 1 Corinthians 9:24–27, Paul compared the believer to a runner in the Greek races. In order to qualify for a crown, he had to obey the rules of the game. If any contestant was found to have disobeyed the rules, he was disqualified and humiliated. The word *castaway* in 1 Corinthians 9:27 does not refer to the loss of salvation, but the loss of reward. "Disqualified" would be a good translation.

Disobeying God's will today may not seem a serious thing, but it will appear very serious when the Lord returns and examines our works (Col. 3:22–25).

3. OBEYING GOD'S WILL (4:15)

"If the Lord will" is not just a statement on a believer's lips; it is the constant attitude of his heart. "My food," said Jesus, "is to do the will of him who sent me and to finish his work" (John 4:34). Often in his letters, Paul referred to the will of God as he shared his plans with his friends (Rom. 1:10; 15:32; 1 Cor. 4:19; 16:7). Paul did not consider the will of God a chain that shackled him; rather, it was a key that opened doors and set him free.

Everything in this universe operates according to laws. If we cooperate with these laws and obey them, then the universe works *with* us. But if we fight these laws and disobey them, the universe will work *against* us. For example, certain laws govern flight. The engineer who obeys those laws in designing and building the plane and the pilot who obeys those laws in flying the plane will both have the joy of seeing the great machine operate perfectly. But if they disobey the basic laws that govern flight, the result will be a crash and the loss of life and money.

God's will for our lives is comparable to the laws He has built within the universe, with this exception: Those laws are general, but the will He has planned for our lives is specifically designed for us. No two lives are planned according to the same pattern.

To be sure, there are some things that must be true of all Christians. It is God's will that we yield ourselves to Him (2 Cor. 8:5). It is God's will that we avoid sexual immorality (1 Thess. 4:3). All Christians should rejoice, pray, and thank God (1 Thess. 5:16–18). Every commandment in the Bible addressed to believers is part of the will of God and must be obeyed. But God does not call each of us to the same work in life, or to exercise the same gifts and ministry. The will of God is "tailor-made" for each of us!

It is important that we have the right attitude toward the will of God. Some people think God's will is a cold, impersonal machine. God starts it going and it is up to us to keep it functioning smoothly. If we disobey Him in some way, the machine grinds to a halt, and we are out of God's will for the rest of our lives.

God's will is not a cold, impersonal machine. You do not determine God's will in some mechanical way, like getting a soft drink out of a vending machine. *The will of God is a living relationship between God and the believer.* This relationship is not *destroyed* when the believer disobeys, for the Father still deals with His child, even if He must chasten.

Rather than looking at the will of God as a cold, impersonal machine, I prefer to see it as a warm, growing, living body. If something goes wrong with my body, I don't die; the other parts of the body compensate for it until I get that organ working properly again. There is pain; there is also weakness; but there is not necessarily death.

When you and I get out of God's will, it is not the end of everything. We suffer, to be sure, but when God cannot rule, He overrules. Just as the body compensates for the malfunctioning of one part, so God adjusts things to bring us back into His will. You see this illustrated clearly in the lives of Abraham and Jonah.

The believer's relationship to the will of God is a growing experience. First, we should *know His will* (Acts 22:14). The will of God is not difficult to discover. If we are willing to obey, He is willing to reveal (John 7:17). It has been said that "obedience is the organ of spiritual knowledge." This is true. God does not reveal His will to the curious or the careless, but to those who are ready and willing to obey Him.

But we must not stop with knowing merely *some* of God's will. God wants us to be "filled with the knowledge of his will and all wisdom and spiritual understanding" (Col. 1:9). It is wrong to want to know God's will about some matters and ignore His will in other matters. Everything in our lives is important to God, and He has a plan for each detail.

God wants us to *understand His will* (Eph. 5:17). This is where spiritual wisdom comes in. A child can *know* the will of his father, but he may not *understand* his will. The child knows the "what" but not the "why." As the "friends" of Jesus Christ, we have the privilege of knowing why God does what He does (John 15:15). "He made known his ways unto Moses, his acts unto the children of Israel" (Ps. 103:7). The Israelites knew *what* God was doing, but Moses understood *why* He was doing it.

We must also *prove God's will* (Rom. 12:2). The Greek verb means "to prove by experience." We learn to determine the will of God by working at it. The more we obey, the easier it is to discover what God wants us to do. It is something like learning to swim or play a musical instrument. You eventually "get the feel" of what you are doing, and it becomes second nature to you.

People who keep asking, "How do I determine God's will for my life?" may be announcing to everybody that they have never really tried to do God's will. You start with the thing you know you ought to do, and you do that. Then God opens the way for the next step. You prove by experience what the will of God is. We learn both from successes and failures. "Take my yoke upon you, and learn of me" (Matt. 11:29). The yoke suggests doing things together, putting into practice what God has taught you.

Finally, we must *do God's will from the heart* (Eph. 6:6). Jonah knew the will of God, and (after a spanking) did the will of God, but he did not do it from his heart. Jonah 4 indicates that the angry prophet did not love the Lord, nor did he love the people of Nineveh. He merely did God's will to keep from getting another spanking!

What Paul said about giving can also be applied to living: "not grudgingly, or of necessity: for God loveth a cheerful giver" (2 Cor. 9:7). *Grudgingly* means "reluctantly, painfully." They get absolutely no joy out of doing God's will. *Of necessity* means "under compulsion." These people obey because they have to, not because they want to. Their heart is not in it.

The secret of a happy life is to delight in duty. When duty becomes delight, then burdens become blessings. "Thy statutes have been my songs in the house of my pilgrimage" (Ps. 119:54). When we love God, then His statutes become songs, and we enjoy serving Him. When we serve God grudgingly, or because we have to, we may accomplish His work but we ourselves will miss the blessing. It will be toil, not ministry. But when we do God's will from the heart, we are enriched, no matter how difficult the task might have been.

We must never think that a failure in knowing or doing God's will permanently affects our relationship with the Lord. We can confess our sins and receive His forgiveness (1 John 1:9). We can learn from the mistakes. The important thing is a heart that loves God and wants sincerely to do His will and glorify His name.

What are the benefits of doing the will of God? For one thing, you enjoy a deeper fellowship with Jesus Christ (Mark 3:35). You have the privilege of knowing God's truth (John 7:17) and seeing your prayers answered (1 John 5:14–15). There is an eternal quality to the life and works of the one who does the will of God (1 John 2:15–17). Certainly, there is the expectation of reward at the return of Jesus Christ (Matt. 25:34).

Which of these three attitudes do you have toward the will of God? Do you totally ignore God's will as you make your daily plans and decisions? Or, do you know God's will and yet refuse to obey it? Each attitude is wrong and can only bring sorrow and ruin to the life of the person who holds it.

But the Christian who knows, loves, and obeys the will of God will enjoy God's blessing. His life may not be easier, but it will be holier and happier. His very food will be the will of God (John 4:34); it will be the joy and delight of his heart (Ps. 40:8).

QUESTIONS FOR PERSONAL REFLECTION
OR GROUP DISCUSSION

1. Why don't we need to be afraid of the will of God?

2. Why is it foolish to ignore the will of God?

3. What is the difference between wasting, spending, or investing our lives? How would you rate yourself in these areas?

4. Why do you think someone who knew the will of God would deliberately disobey it?

5. How detailed do you think the will of God is for you? How can you get to know more of it?

6. How is God's will like a living body?

7. What precondition is there to knowing God's will?

8. What does it mean to "prove" God's will?

9. What does Wiersbe say is the secret to a happy life?

10. What are the benefits of doing the will of God? How can you better seek them in your own life?

Chapter Eleven

MONEY TALKS

(James 5:1–6)

I f money talks," said a popular comedian, "all it ever says to me is good-bye!" But money was not saying good-bye to the men James addressed in this section of his letter. These men were rich, and their riches were sinful. They were using their wealth for selfish purposes and were persecuting the poor in the process.

One of the themes that runs through James 5 is "trouble." We meet poor people deprived of their wages (James 5:4), as well as people who are physically afflicted (James 5:13–16) and spiritually backslidden (James 5:19–20). A second theme that James introduced is "prayer." The poor laborers cry out to God (James 5:4). The sick and afflicted should pray (James 5:13–16). He cited Elijah as an example of one who believed in prayer (James 5:17–18).

When you join these two themes, you arrive at the fifth mark of the mature Christian: *He is prayerful in troubles.* Instead of giving up when troubles come, the mature believer turns to God in prayer and seeks divine help. The immature person trusts in his own experience and skill, or else turns to others for help. While it is true that God often meets our needs through the hands of other people, this aid must be the result of prayer.

James did not say it was a sin to be rich. After all, Abraham was a wealthy man, yet he walked with God and was greatly used of God to bless the whole world. James was concerned about the selfishness of the rich and advised them to "weep and howl." He gave three reasons for his exhortation.

1. THE WAY THEY GOT THEIR WEALTH (5:4, 6A)

The Bible does not discourage the acquiring of wealth. In the law of Moses, specific rules are laid down for getting and securing wealth. The Jews in Canaan owned their own property, worked it, and benefited from the produce. In several of His parables, Jesus indicated His respect for personal property and private gain. There is nothing in the Epistles that contradicts the right of private ownership and profit.

What the Bible does condemn is acquiring wealth by illegal means or for illegal purposes. The prophet Amos thundered a message of judgment against the wealthy upper crust who robbed the poor and used their stolen wealth for selfish luxuries. Isaiah and Jeremiah also exposed the selfishness of the rich and warned that judgment was coming. It is in this spirit that James wrote. He gave two illustrations of how the rich acquired their wealth.

(1) **Holding back wages (v. 4).** Laborers were hired and paid by the day and did not have any legal contracts with their employers. The parable of the laborers in Matthew 20:1–16 gives some idea of the system in that day. In the law, God gave definite instructions concerning the laboring man in order to protect him from the oppressive employer.

"You shall not oppress a hired servant who is poor and needy, whether he is one of your countrymen or one of your aliens who is in your land in your towns. You shall give him his wages on his day before the sun sets, for he is poor and sets his heart on it; so that he will not cry against you to the LORD and it become sin in you" (Deut. 24:14–15 NASB).

"You shall not oppress your neighbor, nor rob him. The wages of a hired man are not to remain with you all night until morning" (Lev. 19:13 NASB).

"Woe unto him that buildeth his house by unrighteousness, and his chambers by wrong; that useth his neighbor's service without wages, and giveth him not for his work" (Jer. 22:13).

These rich men had hired the laborers and promised to pay them a specific amount. The men had completed their work but had not been paid. The tense of the verb "kept back" in the original Greek indicates that the laborers *never will get their salaries.*

"Thou shalt not steal" is still the law of God, and it is a law He will enforce. As Christians, it behooves us to be faithful to pay our bills. As a pastor, I find myself embarrassed when unsaved men tell me about Christians who owe them money and apparently have no intention of paying.

I recall meeting a doctor friend while I was visiting in the hospital. "How are things going?" I asked, and he replied, "Oh, I guess things are okay."

"I pray for you," I told him, wanting to be an encouragement.

"I appreciate that," he replied. "But while you're at it, pray for all the people who owe me money. It'd help if they would pay up!"

(2) Controlling the courts (v. 6a). It is often the case that those who have wealth also have political power and can get what they want. "What is the Golden Rule?" asked a character in a comic strip. His friend answered, "Whoever has the gold makes the rules!" James asked, "Do not rich men oppress you, and draw you before the judgment seats?" (James 2:6).

When the name *Watergate* is mentioned, nobody thinks of a beautiful hotel. That word reminds us of an ugly episode in American history that led to the revelation of lies and the resignation of the president of the United States. Each side accused the other of obstructing justice and manipulating the laws.

When God established Israel in her land, He gave the people a system of courts (see Deut. 17:8–13). He warned the judges not to be greedy (Ex. 18:21). They were not to be partial to the rich or the poor (Lev. 19:15). No judge was to tolerate perjury (Deut. 19:16–21). Bribery was condemned by the Lord (Isa. 33:15; Mic. 3:11; 7:3). The prophet Amos denounced the judges in his day who took bribes and "fixed" cases (Amos 5:12, 15).

The courts in James' day were apparently easy to control if you had enough money. The poor workers could not afford expensive lawsuits, so they were beaten down every time. The workers had the just cause, but they were not given justice. Instead, they were abused and ruined. ("Killed" should probably be taken in a figurative way, as in James 4:2, though it is possible that the rich men could so oppress the poor that the poor would die.) The poor man did not resist the rich man because he had no weapons with which to fight. All he could do was call on the Lord for justice.

The Bible warns us against the securing of wealth by illegal means. God owns all wealth (Ps. 50:10); He permits us to be stewards of His wealth for His glory. "Wealth obtained by fraud dwindles, but the one who gathers by labor increases it" (Prov. 13:11 NASB). It is "the hand of the diligent [that] maketh rich" (Prov. 10:4). "Do not weary yourself to gain wealth" (Prov. 23:4 NASB). We must put God first in our lives, and He will see to it that we always have all that we need (Matt. 6:33).

2. THE WAY THE RICH USED THEIR WEALTH (5:3–5)

It is bad enough to gain wealth in a sinful way, but to use that wealth in sinful ways just makes the sin greater.

They stored it up (v. 3). Of course, there is nothing sinful about saving. "For the children ought not to lay up for the parents, but the parents for the children" (2 Cor. 12:14). "But if any provide not for his own, and specially for those of his own house, he hath denied the faith, and is worse than an infidel" (1 Tim. 5:8). "Then you ought to have put my money in the bank, and on my arrival I would have received my money back with interest" (Matt. 25:27 NASB).

But it is wrong to store up wealth when you owe money to your employees. These rich men were hoarding grain, gold, and garments. They thought that they were rich because they had these possessions. Instead of laying up treasures in heaven by using their wealth for God's glory (Matt. 6:19ff.), they were selfishly guarding it for their own security and pleasure. Not more than ten years after James wrote this letter, Jerusalem fell to the Romans, and all this accumulated wealth was taken.

What did Jesus mean by "laying up treasures in heaven"? Did He mean we should "sell everything and give to the poor" as He instructed the rich young ruler? I think not. He spoke that way to the rich ruler because covetousness was the young man's besetting sin, and Jesus wanted to expose it. To lay up treasures in heaven means to use all that we have as stewards of God's wealth. You and I may *possess* many things, but we do not *own* them. God is the Owner of everything, and we are His stewards.

What we possess and use are merely things, apart from the will of God. When we yield to His will and use what He gives us to serve Him, then things become treasures and we are investing in eternity. What we do on earth is recorded in heaven, and God keeps the books and pays the interest.

What a tragedy it is to see people "heap up treasures for the last days" instead of "laying up treasures in heaven." The Bible does not discourage saving, or even investing; but it does condemn hoarding.

They kept others from benefiting from it (v. 4). By fraudulent means, the rich men robbed the poor. The rich men were not using their own wealth, but they would not pay their laborers and permit them to use the wealth. Perhaps they were waiting for salaries to go down.

Since we are stewards of God's wealth, we have certain responsibilities toward our Master. We must be faithful to use what He gives us for the good of others and the glory of God. "Moreover it is required in stewards, that a man be found faithful" (1 Cor. 4:2). Joseph was a faithful steward in Potiphar's house, and Potiphar prospered. There are ways that we can use God's wealth to help others.

They lived in luxury (v. 5). "You have lived in high style on the earth!" (James 5:5, literal translation). Luxury is waste, and waste is sin.

A magazine advertisement told of the shopping spree of an oil-rich sultan. He purchased nineteen Cadillacs, one for each of his nineteen wives, and paid extra to have the cars lengthened. He also bought two Porsches, six Mercedes, a $40,000 speedboat, and a truck for hauling it. Add to the list sixteen refrigerators, $47,000 worth of women's luggage, two Florida grapefruit trees, two reclining chairs, and one slot machine. His total bill was $1.5 million, and he had to pay another $194,500 to have everything delivered. Talk about living in luxury!

All of us are grateful for the good things of life, and we would certainly not want to return to primitive conditions. But we recognize the fact that there is a point of diminishing returns. "Tell me what thou dost need," said the Quaker to his neighbor, "and I will tell thee how to get along without it." Jesus said, "Beware, and be on your guard against every form of greed; for not even when one has an abundance does his life consist of his possessions" (Luke 12:15 NASB). These rich men James addressed were feeding themselves on their riches and starving to death. The Greek word pictures cattle being fattened for the slaughter.

There is a great difference between enjoying what God has given us

(1 Tim. 6:17) and living extravagantly on what we have withheld from others. Even if what we have has been earned lawfully and in the will of God, we must not waste it on selfish living. There are too many needs to be met.

Luxury has a way of ruining character. It is a form of self-indulgence. If you match character with wealth, you can produce much good; but if you match self-indulgence with wealth, the result is sin. The rich man Jesus described in Luke 16:19–31 would have felt right at home with the rich men James wrote to!

3. WHAT THEIR RICHES WILL DO (5:1–4)

The rich thought they had it made because of their wealth, but God thought otherwise. "Howl for your miseries that shall come upon you" (James 5:1). James described the consequences of misusing riches.

Riches will vanish (vv. 2–3a). Grain will rot ("corrupted" in James 5:2); gold will rust; and garments will become moth-eaten. Nothing material in this world will last forever. The seeds of death and decay are found in all of creation.

It is a great mistake to think there is security in wealth. Paul wrote, "Instruct those who are rich in this present world not to be conceited or to fix their hope on the uncertainty of riches" (1 Tim. 6:17 NASB). Riches are uncertain. The money market fluctuates from hour to hour, and so does the stock market. Actually, gold does not rust the way iron does, but the idea is the same: The gold is losing its value. Add to this the fact that life is brief, and we cannot take wealth with us, and you can see how foolish it is to live for the things of this world. God said to the rich man, "Thou fool, this night thy soul shall be required of thee: then whose shall those things be, which thou hast provided?" (Luke 12:20).

Misused riches erode character (v. 3). "Their corrosion will ... eat your flesh like fire" (James 5:3 NIV). This is a present judgment: The poison of wealth has infected them and they are being eaten alive. Of itself, money is not sinful; it is neutral. But "the love of money is the root of all evil" (1 Tim. 6:10). "Thou shalt not covet" is the last of the Ten Commandments, but it is the most dangerous. Covetousness will make a person break all the other nine commandments.

Abraham was a rich man, but he maintained his faith and character. When Lot became rich, it ruined his character and ultimately ruined his family. It is good to have riches in your hand provided they do not get into your heart. "If riches increase, set not your heart upon them" (Ps. 62:10). "A GOOD name is rather to be chosen than great riches, and loving favour rather than silver and gold" (Prov. 22:1).

Judgment is a certainty (vv. 3, 5). James not only saw a *present* judgment (their wealth decaying, their character eroding), but also a *future* judgment before God. Jesus Christ will be the Judge (James 5:9), and His judgment will be righteous.

Note the witnesses that God will call on that day of judgment. First, the rich men's *wealth* will witness against them (James 5:3). Their rotten grain, rusted gold and silver, and moth-eaten garments will bear witness of the selfishness of their hearts. There is a bit of irony here: The rich men saved their wealth to help them, but their hoarded riches will only testify against them.

The *wages* they held back will also witness against them in court (James 5:4a). Money talks! These stolen salaries cry out to God for justice and judgment. God heard Abel's blood cry out from the ground (Gen. 4:10), and He hears this stolen money cry out too.

The *workers* will also testify against them (James 5:4). There will be no opportunities for the rich to bribe the witnesses or the Judge. God hears the cries of His oppressed people and He will judge righteously.

This judgment is a serious thing. The lost will stand before Christ at the

Great White Throne (Rev. 20:11–15). The saved will stand before the judgment seat of Christ (Rom. 14:10–12; 2 Cor. 5:9–10). God will not judge our *sins,* because they have already been judged on the cross, but He will judge our *works* and our ministry. If we have been faithful in serving and glorifying Him, we will receive a reward; if we have been unfaithful, we shall lose our reward but not our salvation (1 Cor. 3:1–15).

The loss of a precious opportunity (v. 3). "The last days" indicates that James believed that the coming of the Lord was near (see James 5:8–9). We must "buy up the opportunity" (Eph. 5:16, literal translation) and work while it is day (John 9:4). Think of the good that could have been accomplished with that hoarded wealth. There were poor people in that congregation who could have been helped (James 2:1–6). There were workers who deserved their wages. Sad to say, in a few years the Jewish nation was defeated and scattered, and Jerusalem destroyed.

It is good to have the things that money can buy, provided you also have the things that money cannot buy. What good is a $500,000 house if there is no home? Or a million-dollar diamond ring if there is no love? James did not condemn riches or rich people; he condemned the wrong use of riches, and rich people who use their wealth as a weapon and not as a tool with which to build.

It is possible to be "poor in this world" (James 2:5) and yet rich in the next world. It is also possible to be "rich in this world" (1 Tim. 6:17) and poor in the next world. The return of Jesus Christ will make some people poor and others rich, depending on the spiritual condition of their hearts. "For where your treasure is, there will your heart be also" (Matt. 6:21).

What we keep, we lose. What we give to God, we keep, and He adds interest to it. A famous preacher, known for his long sermons, was asked to give the annual "charity sermon" for the poor. It was suggested that if he preached too long, the congregation might not give as much as they should.

The preacher read his text from Proverbs 19:17—"He that hath pity upon the poor lendeth unto the LORD; and that which he hath given will he pay him again." His sermon indeed was brief: "If you like the terms, then put down your money."

Yes, money talks. What will it say to you at the last judgment?

QUESTIONS FOR PERSONAL REFLECTION
OR GROUP DISCUSSION

1. How does a mature Christian respond in times of trouble?

2. Why does James admonish the rich to weep and howl?

3. What are the sinful ways the rich use their wealth? How do you use your wealth?

4. What did Jesus mean when He said to lay up treasures in heaven?

5. What is the proper Christian approach to wealth? How do Christians benefit from approaching wealth in this way?

6. What are the consequences of misusing riches?

7. Who will be the witnesses in judgment against the selfish rich?

8. What does the term *stewardship* mean?

9. Where do you draw the line between enjoying what God gives you and living a life of luxury?

10. Is it ever okay to have more material wealth than other believers, or should equality be the goal? Why or why not?

Chapter Twelve

THE POWER OF
PATIENCE

(James 5:7–12)

J ames was still addressing the suffering saints when he wrote, "Be patient." This was his counsel at the beginning of his letter (James 1:1–5) and his counsel as his letter came to a close. God is not going to right all the wrongs in this world until Jesus Christ returns, and we believers must patiently endure—and expect.

Three times James reminded us of the coming of the Lord (James 5:7–9). This is the "blessed hope" of the Christian (Titus 2:13). We do not expect to have everything easy and comfortable in this present life. "In the world ye shall have tribulation" (John 16:33). Paul reminded his converts that "we must through much tribulation enter into the kingdom of God" (Acts 14:22). We must patiently endure hardships and heartaches until Jesus returns.

James used two different words for patience. In James 5:7–8, 10 it was the word *long-tempered*. The words *endure* and *patience* in James 5:11 literally mean "to remain under" and speak of endurance under great stress. *Patience* means "to stay put and stand fast when you'd like to run away." Many Greek scholars think that "longsuffering" refers to patience with respect to persons, while "endurance" refers to patience with respect to conditions or situations.

But the question we must answer is, how can we as Christians experience this kind of patient endurance as we wait for the Lord to return? To answer that question (and need), James gave three encouraging examples of patient endurance.

1. THE FARMER (5:7–9)

If a man is impatient, then he had better not become a farmer. No crop appears overnight (except perhaps a crop of weeds), and no farmer has control over the weather. Too much rain can cause the crop to rot, and too much sun can burn it up. An early frost can kill the crop. How longsuffering the farmer must be with the weather!

He must also have patience with the seed and the crop, for it takes time for plants to grow. Jewish farmers would plow and sow in what to us are the autumn months. The "early rain" would soften the soil. The "latter rain" would come in the early spring (our February-March) and help to mature the harvest. The farmer had to wait many weeks for his seed to produce fruit.

Why did he willingly wait so long? Because the fruit is "precious" (James 5:7). The harvest is worth waiting for. "In due season we shall reap, if we faint not" (Gal. 6:9). "The soil produces crops by itself; first the blade, then the head, then the mature grain in the head. But when the crop permits, he immediately puts in the sickle, because the harvest has come" (Mark 4:28–29 NASB).

James pictured the Christian as a "spiritual farmer" looking for a spiritual harvest. "Be ye also patient, stablish your hearts" (James 5:8). Our hearts are the soil, and the "seed is the word of God" (Luke 8:11). There are seasons to the spiritual life just as there are seasons to the soil. Sometimes our hearts become cold and "wintry," and the Lord has to "plow them up" before He can plant the seed (Jer. 4:3). He sends the sunshine and the rains of His goodness to water and nurture the seeds planted, but we must be patient to wait for the harvest.

Here, then, is a secret of endurance when the going is tough: *God is producing a harvest in our lives.* He wants the "fruit of the Spirit" to grow (Gal. 5:22–23), and the only way He can do it is through trials and troubles. Instead of growing impatient with God and with ourselves, we must yield to the Lord and permit the fruit to grow. We are "spiritual farmers" looking for a harvest.

You can enjoy this kind of a harvest only if your heart is *established* (James 5:8). One of the purposes of the spiritual ministry of the local church is to establish the heart (Rom. 1:11). Paul sent Timothy to Thessalonica to establish the young Christians in their faith (1 Thess. 3:1–3), and Paul also prayed for them that they might be established (1 Thess. 3:10–13). The ministry of the Word of God and prayer are important if the heart is going to be established. A heart that is not established cannot bear fruit.

Keep in mind that the farmer does not stand around doing nothing; he is constantly at work as he looks toward the harvest. James did not tell these suffering believers to put on white robes, climb a hill, and wait for Jesus to return. "Keep working and waiting" was his admonition. "Blessed is that servant, whom his lord when he cometh shall find so doing" (Luke 12:43).

Nor does the farmer get into fights with his neighbors. One of the usual marks of farmers is their willingness to help one another. Nobody on the farm has time or energy for disputes with the neighbors. James must have had this in mind when he added, "Don't grumble against each other, brothers, or you will be judged" (James 5:9 NIV). Impatience with God often leads to impatience with God's people, and this is a sin we must avoid. If we start using the sickles on each other, we will miss the harvest!

2. The Prophets (5:10)

A Jewish congregation would understand this simple reference that James made to the Old Testament prophets. In His Sermon on the Mount, Jesus also used the prophets as an example of victory over persecution (Matt. 5:10–12). What encouragements do we receive from their example?

For one thing, they were in the will of God, yet they suffered. They were preaching "in the name of the Lord," yet they were persecuted. Satan tells the faithful Christian that his suffering is the result of sin or unfaithfulness, and yet his suffering might well be *because of faithfulness!* "Yea, and all that will live godly in Christ Jesus shall suffer persecution" (2 Tim. 3:12). We must never think that obedience automatically produces ease and pleasure. Our Lord was obedient, and it led to a cross!

The prophets encourage us by reminding us that God cares for us when we go through sufferings for His sake. Elijah announced to wicked King Ahab that there would be a drought in the land for three and one-half years, and Elijah himself had to suffer in that drought. But God cared for him, and God gave him victory over the evil priests of Baal. It has been said, "The will of God will never lead you where the grace of God cannot keep you."

Many of the prophets had to endure great trials and sufferings, not only at the hands of unbelievers, but at the hands of professed believers. Jeremiah was arrested as a traitor and even thrown into an abandoned well to die. God fed Jeremiah and protected him throughout that terrible siege of Jerusalem, even though at times it looked as though the prophet was going to be killed. Both Ezekiel and Daniel had their share of hardships, but the Lord delivered them. And even those who were not delivered, who died for the faith, received that special reward for those who are true to Him.

Why is it that those who "speak in the name of the Lord" often must endure difficult trials? It is so that their lives might back up their messages.

The impact of a faithful, godly life carries much power. We need to remind ourselves that our patience in times of suffering is a testimony to others around us.

But have not many faithful Christians suffered and died without any notice or recognition? Yes, but when Jesus returns, these "obscure heroes" will receive their rewards. The prophets were killed and buried, but today their names are honored. When our Lord comes again, He will bring His reward with Him (Rev. 22:12).

This example that James used from the Old Testament prophets ought to encourage us to spend more time in the Bible, getting acquainted with these heroes of faith. "For everything that was written in the past was written to teach us, so that through endurance and the encouragement of the Scriptures we might have hope" (Rom. 15:4 NIV). The better we know the Bible, the more God can encourage us in the difficult experiences of life. The important thing is that, like the farmer, we keep working, and, like the prophets, we keep witnessing, no matter how trying the circumstances may be.

3. JOB (5:11–12)

"As you know, we consider blessed those who have persevered" (James 5:11 NIV). But you cannot persevere unless there is a trial in your life. There can be no victories without battles; there can be no peaks without valleys. If you want the blessing, you must be prepared to carry the burden and fight the battle.

I once heard a young Christian pray, "O Lord, please teach me the deep truths of Thy Word! I want to be lifted up to the heavens to hear and see the wonderful things that are there!" It was a sincere prayer, but the young man did not realize what he was praying. Paul went to the third heaven and learned things too marvelous for words, and as a result, *God had to give Paul a thorn in the flesh to keep him humble* (2 Cor. 12:1–10). God has to balance privileges with responsibilities, blessings with burdens, or else you and I will become spoiled, pampered children.

When do "blessings" come? In the midst of trials we may experience God's blessings, as did the three Hebrew children in the fiery furnace (Dan. 3), but James taught that there is a blessing *after we have endured.* His example was Job.

The book of Job is a long book, and the chapters are filled with speeches that, to the Western mind, seem long and tedious. In the first three chapters you have *Job's distress:* He loses his wealth, his family (except for his wife, and she told him to commit suicide), and his health. In Job 4—31 we read *Job's defense,* as he debates with his three friends and answers their false accusations. Job 38—42 presents *Job's deliverance:* First God humbles Job, and then He honors Job and gives him twice as much as he had before.

In studying the experience of Job, it is important to remember that Job did not know what was going on "behind the scenes" between God and Satan. Job's friends accused him of being a sinner and a hypocrite. "There must be some terrible sin in your life," they argued, "or God would never have permitted this suffering." Job disagreed with them and maintained his innocence (but not perfection) during the entire conversation. The friends were wrong: God had no cause against Job (Job 2:3), and in the end, God rebuked the friends for telling lies about Job (Job 42:7).

It is difficult to find a greater example of suffering than Job. Circumstances were against him, for he lost his wealth and his health. He also lost his beloved children. His wife was against him, for she said, "Curse God and die" (Job 2:9). His friends were against him, for they accused him of being a hypocrite, deserving of the judgment of God. And it seemed like God was against him! When Job cried out for answers to his questions, there was no reply from heaven.

Yet, Job endured. Satan predicted that Job would get impatient with God and abandon his faith, but that did not happen. It is true that Job questioned God's will, but Job did not forsake his faith in the Lord. "Though He slay me, I will hope in Him. Nevertheless, I will argue my ways before Him" (Job 13:15 NASB). Job was so sure of God's perfections that he persisted in arguing with Him, even though he did not understand all that God was doing. That is endurance.

God made a covenant with Israel that He would bless them if they would obey His laws (see Deut. 11). This led to the idea that, if you were wealthy and comfortable, you were blessed of God, but if you were suffering and poor, you were cursed of God. Sad to say, many people have that same erroneous idea today. When Jesus said it was difficult for a rich man to enter heaven, the disciples were shocked. "Who then can be saved?" they asked (Matt. 19:23–26). "The rich are especially blessed of God," they were saying. "If *they* can't make it, nobody can!"

The book of Job refutes that idea, for Job was a righteous man, *and yet he suffered.* God found no evil in him, and even Satan could not find any. Job's friends could not prove their accusations. Job teaches us that God has higher purposes in suffering than the punishing of sin. Job's experience paved the way for Jesus, the perfect Son of God who suffered, not for His own sins, but for the sins of the world.

In Job's case, what was "the end [purpose] of the Lord"? *To reveal Himself as full of pity and tender mercy.* Certainly, there were other results from Job's experience, for God never wastes the sufferings of His saints. Job met God in a new and deeper way (Job 42:1–6), and after that, Job received greater blessings from the Lord.

"But if God is so merciful," someone may argue, "why didn't He protect Job from all that suffering to begin with?" To be sure, there are mysteries to God's working that our finite minds cannot fathom, but this we know:

God was glorified and Job was purified through this difficult experience. If there is nothing to endure, you cannot learn endurance.

What did Job's story mean to the believers James wrote to, and what does it mean to us today? It means that some of the trials of life are caused directly by satanic opposition. God permits Satan to try His children, but He always limits the extent of the enemy's power (Job 1:12; 2:6). When you find yourself in the fire, remember that God keeps His gracious hand on the thermostat! "But he knoweth the way that I take: when he hath tried me, I shall come forth as gold" (Job 23:10).

Satan wants us to get impatient with God, for an impatient Christian is a powerful weapon in the Devil's hands. You will recall from our study of James 1 that Moses' impatience robbed him of a trip to the Holy Land; Abraham's impatience led to the birth of Ishmael, the enemy of the Jews; and Peter's impatience almost made him a murderer. When Satan attacks us, it is easy for us to get impatient and run ahead of God and lose God's blessing as a result.

What is the answer? "My grace is sufficient for thee" (2 Cor. 12:7–9)! Paul's thorn in the flesh was a "messenger of Satan." Paul could have fought it, given up under it, or tried to deny that the thorn existed; but he did not. Instead, he trusted God for the grace he needed, and he turned Satan's weapon into a tool for the building up of his own spiritual life.

When you find yourself in the furnace, go to the throne of grace and receive from the Lord all the grace you need to endure (Heb. 4:14–16). Remind yourself that the Lord has a gracious purpose in all of this suffering, and that He will work out His purposes in His time and for His glory. You are not a robot caught in the jaws of fate. You are a loving child of God, privileged to be a part of a wonderful plan. There is a difference!

The exhortation in James 5:12 seems out of place, for what does "speaking oaths" have to do with the problem of suffering? If you have ever suffered, you know the answer: It is easy to say things you do not mean, and even make bargains with God, when you are going through difficulties. Go back to Job for an example. The patriarch said, "Naked came I out of my mother's womb, and naked shall I return thither: the LORD gave, and the LORD hath taken away; blessed be the name of the LORD. In all this Job sinned not, nor charged God foolishly" (Job 1:21–22). Job did curse the day he was born (Job 3:1ff.), but he never cursed God or spoke with a foolish oath. Neither did he try to bargain with God.

Surely James was reminding us of our Lord's teaching in the Sermon on the Mount (Matt. 5:34–37). The Jews were great ones for using various oaths to back up their statements. They were careful, however, not to use the name of God in their oaths, lest they blaspheme God. So, they would swear by heaven, or earth, or Jerusalem, or even by their own heads! But Jesus taught that it is impossible to avoid God in such oaths. Heaven is His throne, earth is His footstool, and Jerusalem is the "city of the great King." As for swearing by your head, what good is it? "Thou canst not make one hair black or white" (Matt. 5:36)—or even keep one hair on your head.

It is a basic principle that true Christian character requires few words. The person who must use many words (including oaths) to convince us has something wrong with his character and must bolster this weakness by using words. If you are a true Christian, with integrity, then all you have to say is yes or no and people will believe you. Jesus warned us that anything more than this is from the evil one.

One of the purposes of suffering is the building of character. Certainly Job was a better man for having gone through the furnace. (James explained this process to us, James 1:2–12.) If words are a test of character, then oaths would indicate that there is yet work to be done. When Peter poured out those oaths in the courtyard (Matt. 26:71), he was giving evidence that his character was still in need of a transformation.

As you review this section, you can see the practicality of it. James wanted to encourage us to be patient in times of suffering. Like the farmer, we are waiting for a spiritual harvest, for fruit that will glorify God. Like the prophets, we look for opportunities for witness, to share the truth of God. And, like Job, we wait for the Lord to fulfill His loving purpose, knowing that He will never cause His children to suffer needlessly. And, like Job, we shall have a clearer vision of the Lord and come to know Him better for having been in the furnace of affliction.

"Be patient, for the coming of the Lord draweth nigh!"

QUESTIONS FOR PERSONAL REFLECTION
OR GROUP DISCUSSION

1. How can Christians find patient endurance as they wait for Christ to return?

2. What three examples of patience does James give? Which of these resonates with you? Why?

3. How are we like "spiritual farmers"?

4. What do the soil, seed, seasons, and harvest typify?

5. Where in this illustration is the secret to endurance?

6. As we read of the prophets, what encouragement do we gain?

7. Why do faithful witnesses to God often undergo suffering and persecution? Where is their reward?

8. What does God accomplish in Christians through suffering?

9. What meaning can the book of Job have for Christians today?

10. What should you do (or not do) when you find yourself in the midst of suffering?

Chapter Thirteen

LET US PRAY

(James 5:13–20)

he gift of speech is a marvelous blessing, if it is used to the glory of God. As we have seen, James had a great deal to say about the tongue, and this chapter is no exception. He mentioned some of the lowest uses of the tongue: complaining (James 5:9) and swearing (James 5:12). But he also named some of the highest uses of the tongue: proclaiming God's Word (James 5:10) and praying and praising God (James 5:13).

Prayer is certainly a high and holy privilege. To think that, as God's children, we can come freely and boldly to His throne and share with Him our needs! Seven times in this section James mentioned prayer. The mature Christian is prayerful in the troubles of life. Instead of complaining about his situation, he talks to God about it, and God hears and answers his prayers. "Taking it to the Lord in prayer" is certainly a mark of spiritual maturity.

In this section, James encouraged us to pray by describing four situations in which God answers prayer.

1. PRAYER FOR THE SUFFERING (5:13)

The word *afflicted* means "suffering in difficult circumstances." The phrase "in trouble" is a good translation. Paul used this word to describe the circumstances he was in as he suffered for the gospel's sake (2 Tim. 2:9). As God's people go through life, they often must endure difficulties that are not the results of sin or the chastening of God.

What should we do when we find ourselves in such trying circumstances? We must not grumble and criticize the saints who are having an easier time of it (James 5:9), nor should we blame the Lord. We should pray, asking God for the wisdom we need to understand the situation and use it to His glory (James 1:5).

Prayer can remove affliction, if that is God's will. But prayer can also give us the grace we need to endure troubles and use them to accomplish God's perfect will. *God can transform troubles into triumphs.* "He giveth more grace" (James 4:6). Paul prayed that God might change his circumstances, but instead, God gave Paul the grace he needed to turn his weakness into strength (2 Cor. 12:7–10). Our Lord prayed in Gethsemane that the cup might be removed, and it was not, yet the Father gave Him the strength He needed to go to the cross and die for our sins.

James indicated that everybody does not go through troubles at the same time: "Is any merry? Let him sing psalms" (James 5:13). God balances our lives and gives us hours of suffering and days of singing. The mature Christian knows how to sing *while he is suffering.* (Anybody can sing after the trouble has passed.) God is able to give "songs in the night" (Job 35:10). He did this for Paul and Silas when they were suffering in that Philippian jail. "And at midnight Paul and Silas prayed, and sang praises unto God" (Acts 16:25).

Praying and singing were important elements in worship in the early church, and they should be important to us. Our singing ought to be an expression of our inner spiritual life. The believer's praise should be intelligent (1 Cor. 14:15) and not just the mouthing of words or ideas that mean nothing to him. It should come from the heart (Eph. 5:19) and be motivated by the Holy Spirit (Eph. 5:18). Christian singing must be based on the Word of God (Col. 3:16) and not simply on the clever ideas of men. If a song is not biblical, it is not acceptable to God.

2. Prayer for the Sick (5:14–16)

I do not think that James gave us a blanket formula for healing the sick. In the churches I have pastored, the elders and I have prayed for the sick, and sometimes God has given healing. But other times He has not seen fit to heal the person. I recall two cases within one week of each other: The one woman was restored in an almost miraculous way, but the other one had to enter the hospital for surgery, and eventually the Lord called her home.

What are the special characteristics of this case that James was describing?

The person is sick because of sin (vv. 15b–16). The Greek text says, "If he has been constantly sinning." This parallels 1 Corinthians 11:30: "For this cause many are weak and sickly among you, and many sleep" (have died). James has described a church member who is sick because he is being disciplined by God. This explains why the elders of the assembly are called: The man cannot go to church to confess his sins, so he asks the spiritual leaders to come to him. The leaders would be in charge of the discipline of the congregation.

The person confesses his sins (v. 16). In the early church, the believers practiced church discipline. First Corinthians 5 is a good example. Paul told the believers at Corinth to dismiss the sinning member from the assembly until he repented of his sins and made things right. The little word *therefore* belongs in James 5:16—"Confess your sins therefore to one another, and pray for one another, that you may be healed" (literal translation). The word *faults* in the Authorized Version gives the impression that the man's deeds were not too evil; they were only faults. But it is the word *hamartia* that James used, and this word means "sin." It is the same word used in James 1:15, where the subject is definitely sin.

The person is healed by "the prayer of faith" (v. 15). It is not the anointing that heals, but the praying. The Greek word translated "anointing" is a medicinal term; it could be translated "massaging." This may be an indication that James suggests using available means for healing along with asking the Lord for His divine touch. God can heal with or without means; in each case, it is God who does the healing.

But what is "the prayer of faith" that heals the sick? The answer is in 1 John 5:14–15—"And this is the confidence that we have in him, that, if we ask anything according to his will, he heareth us: and if we know that he hear us, whatsoever we ask, we know that we have the petitions that we desired of him." The "prayer of faith" is a prayer offered *when you know the will of God.* The elders would seek the mind of God in the matter, and then pray according to His will.

As I visited the sick among my congregation, I did not always know how to pray for them. (Paul had the same problem; read Rom. 8:26.) Was it God's will to heal? Was God planning to call His child home? I did not know; therefore, I had to pray, "If it is Your will, heal Your child." Those who claim that God heals every case, and that it is not His will for His children to be sick, are denying both Scripture and experience. But where we have the inner conviction from the Word and the Spirit that it is God's will to heal, then we can pray "the prayer of faith" and expect God to work.

Keep in mind that it is not one individual who is praying: It is the body of elders—spiritual men of God—who seek God's will and pray. James did not instruct the believer to send for a faith healer. The matter is in the hands of the leaders of the local church.

There are some practical lessons from this section that we must not overlook. For one thing, disobedience to God can lead to sickness. This was

David's experience when he tried to hide his sins (Ps. 32). Second, sin affects the whole church. We can never sin alone, for sin has a way of growing and infecting others. This man had to confess his sins to the church because he had sinned against the church. Third, there is healing (physical and spiritual) when sin is dealt with. "He that covereth his sins shall not prosper: but whoso confesseth and forsaketh them shall have mercy" (Prov. 28:13). James wrote, "Make it a habit to confess your sins to each other" (literal translation). Do not hide sin or delay confession.

The "confessing" that James wrote about is done among the saints. He was not suggesting confessing our sins to a preacher or priest. We confess our sins first of all to the Lord (1 John 1:9), but we must also confess them to those who have been affected by them. *We must never confess sin beyond the circle of that sin's influence.* Private sin requires private confession; public sin requires public confession. It is wrong for Christians to "hang dirty wash in public," for such "confessing" might do more harm than the original sin.

3. PRAYER FOR THE NATION (5:17–18)

James cited Elijah as an example of a "righteous man" whose prayers released power. "The prayer of a righteous man is powerful and effective" (James 5:16 NIV).

The background of this incident is found in 1 Kings 17—18. Wicked King Ahab and Jezebel, his queen, had led Israel away from the Lord and into the worship of Baal. God punished the nation by holding back the rain that they needed (see Deut. 28:12, 23). For three and one-half years, the heavens were as brass and the earth unable to produce the crops so necessary for life.

Then Elijah challenged the priests of Baal on Mount Carmel. All day long the priests cried out to their god, but no answer came. At the time of the evening sacrifice, Elijah repaired the altar and prepared the sacrifice. He prayed but once, and fire came from heaven to consume the sacrifice. He had proven that Jehovah was the true God.

But the nation still needed rain. Elijah went to the top of Carmel and fell down before the Lord in prayer. He prayed and sent his servant seven times to see if there was evidence of rain, and the seventh time his servant saw a little cloud. Before long, there was a great rain, and the nation was saved.

Do we need "showers of blessing" today? We certainly do!

"But Elijah was a special prophet of God," we might argue. "We can expect God to answer his prayers in a wonderful way."

"Elijah was a man just like us," stated James (5:17 NIV). He was not perfect; in fact, right after his victory on Mount Carmel, Elijah became afraid and discouraged and ran away. But he was a "righteous man," that is, obedient to the Lord and trusting Him. God's promises of answered prayer are for all His children, not just for ones we may call the spiritual elite.

Elijah prayed in faith, for God told him He would send the rain (1 Kings 18:1). "Prayer," said Robert Law, "is not getting man's will done in heaven. It's getting God's will done on earth." You cannot separate the Word of God and prayer, for in His Word He gives us the promises that we claim when we pray.

Elijah was not only believing in his praying, but he was persistent. "He prayed … and he prayed again" (James 5:17–18). On Mount Carmel, Elijah continued to pray for rain until his servant reported "a cloud the size of a man's hand." Too many times we fail to get what God promises because we stop praying. It is true that we are not heard "for our much praying" (Matt. 6:7), but there is a difference between vain repetitions and true believing persistence in prayer. Our Lord prayed three times in the garden, and Paul prayed three times that his thorn in the flesh might be taken from him.

Elijah was determined and concerned in his praying. "He prayed earnestly" (James 5:17 NIV). The literal Greek reads, "and he prayed in prayer." Many people do not pray in their prayers. They just lazily say religious words, and their hearts are not in their prayers.

A church member was "praying around the world" in a prayer meeting, and one of the men present was growing tired of the speech. Finally the man cried out, "Ask Him something!" That is what prayer is all about: "Ask Him something!"

Prayer power is the greatest power in the world today. "Tremendous power is made available through a good man's earnest prayer" (James 5:16 PH). History shows how mankind has progressed from manpower to horsepower, and then to dynamite and TNT, and now to nuclear power.

But greater than nuclear power is prayer power. Elijah prayed for his nation, and God answered prayer. We need to pray for our nation today, that God will bring conviction and revival, and that "showers of blessing" will come to the land. One of the first responsibilities of the local church is to pray for government leaders (1 Tim. 2:1–3).

4. PRAYER FOR THE STRAYING (5:19–20)

While James did not specifically name prayer in these verses, the implication is there. If we pray for the afflicted and the sick, surely we must pray for the brother who wanders from the truth.

These verses deal with our ministry to a fellow believer who strays from the truth and gets into sin. The verb *err* means "to wander," and suggests a gradual moving away from the will of God. The Old Testament term for this is "backsliding." Sad to say, we see this tragedy occurring in our churches regularly. Sometimes a brother is "overtaken in a fault" (Gal. 6:1), but usually the sin is the result of slow, gradual spiritual decline.

Such a condition is, of course, very dangerous. It is dangerous to the offender because he may be disciplined by the Lord (Heb. 12). He also faces the danger of committing "sin unto death" (1 John 5:16–17). God disciplined the sinning members of the Corinthian church, even to the point of taking some of them to heaven (1 Cor. 11:30).

But this backsliding is also dangerous to the church. A wandering offender can influence others and lead them astray. "One sinner destroys much good" (Eccl. 9:18 NASB). This is why the spiritual members of the church must step in and help the man who has wandered away.

The *origin of this problem* is found in the statement "wander from the truth" (James 5:19). The *truth* means, of course, the Word of God. "Thy word is truth" (John 17:17). Unless the believer stays close to the truth, he will start to drift away. "For this reason we must pay much closer attention to what we have heard, so that we do not drift away from it" (Heb. 2:1 NASB). Jesus warned Peter that Satan was at hand to tempt him, and Peter refused to believe the Word. He even argued with the Lord! When he should have been praying, Peter was sleeping. No wonder he denied three times.

The *outcome* of this wandering is "sin" and possible "death" (James 5:20). The sinner here is a believer, not an unbeliever; and sin in the life of a Christian is worse than sin in the life of an unbeliever. We expect unsaved people to sin, but God expects His children to obey His Word.

What are we to do when we see a fellow believer wandering from the truth? We should pray for him, to be sure, but we must also seek to help him. He needs to be "converted"—turned back into the right path again. Do believers need to be converted? Yes, they do! Jesus said to Peter, "When thou art converted, strengthen thy brethren" (Luke 22:32).

It is important that we seek to win the lost, but it is also important to win the saved. If a brother has sinned against us, we should talk to him privately and seek to settle the matter. If he listens, then we have gained our brother (Matt. 18:15). That word *gained* means "won." It is the same word translated "get gain" in James 4:13. It is important to win the saved as well as the lost.

If we are going to help an erring brother, we must have an attitude of love, for "love shall cover the multitude of sins" (1 Peter 4:8). Both James and Peter learned this principle from Proverbs 10:12—"Hate stirreth up strifes: but love covereth all sins."

This does not mean that love "sweeps the dirt under the carpet." Where there is love, there must also be truth ("speaking the truth in love," said Paul in Eph. 4:15), and where there is truth, there is honest confession of sin and cleansing from God. Love not only helps the offender to face his sins and deal with them, but love also assures the offender that those sins, once forgiven, are remembered no more.

While the basic interpretation of these verses is as I have explained, the application can be made to the lost sinner. After all, if a straying brother needs to be restored, how much more does a lost sinner need to be brought to the Savior. If the wandering believer loses his life, he at least goes to heaven, but the lost sinner is condemned to an eternal hell.

"Seeking the lost" is a common Bible picture of soul winning. In Luke 15, Jesus pictured the lost sheep, the lost coin, and the lost son, all of whom needed to be found and brought back to where they belonged. Our Lord also compared winning souls to catching fish (Mark 1:17). Peter caught one fish individually with his hook (Matt. 17:24–27), but he also worked with his helpers and used the nets to catch many fish at one time. There is a place for both personal and collective evangelism.

Proverbs 11:30 compares evangelism to hunting: "He that catcheth souls is wise" (literal translation). Sin is out to catch and kill (James 1:13–15), but we ought to be out to catch and make alive.

The soul winner is also an ambassador of peace (2 Cor. 5:20). God has not declared war on this world; He has declared peace! One day He will declare war, and judgment will fall.

Both Zechariah 3:2 and Jude 23 picture the soul winner as a fireman, pulling brands out of the burning. John Wesley applied Zechariah 3:2 to himself, for when he was but a child, he was pulled from a burning house when it looked as though it was too late. Sometimes we must take risks of love to snatch people from the fires of judgment.

Jesus compared evangelism to sowing and reaping (John 4:34–38) and Paul used the same illustration (1 Cor. 3:6–9). There are seasons of sowing and seasons of reaping; and many people are needed for the work. We are "laborers together with God" (1 Cor. 3:9). Both the sower and the reaper will receive their rewards, for there is no competition in the Lord's fields.

This brings us to the end of our study of James. His emphasis has been spiritual maturity. This would be a good time for us to examine our own hearts to see how mature we really are. Here are a few questions to assist you:

1. Am I becoming more and more patient in the testings of life?

2. Do I play with temptation or resist it from the start?

3. Do I find joy in obeying the Word of God, or do I merely study it and learn it?

4. Are there any prejudices that shackle me?

5. Am I able to control my tongue?

6. Am I a peacemaker rather than a troublemaker? Do people come to me for spiritual wisdom?

7. Am I a friend of God or a friend of the world?

8. Do I make plans without considering the will of God?

9. Am I selfish when it comes to money? Am I unfaithful in the paying of my bills?

10. Do I naturally depend on prayer when I find myself in some kind of trouble?

11. Am I the kind of person others seek for prayer support?

12. What is my attitude toward the wandering brother? Do I criticize and gossip, or do I seek to restore him in love?

Don't just grow old— grow up! Be mature!

QUESTIONS FOR PERSONAL REFLECTION
OR GROUP DISCUSSION

1. What were the specific circumstances surrounding the prayer offered for the sick in James 5:14–16?

2. What is "the prayer of faith"?

3. What part should modern medicine have in healing our illnesses? Why?

4. What damage can be done if sin is confessed beyond the circle of its influence?

5. Why is it impossible to separate the Word of God and prayer?

6. What is the difference between the "much praying" mentioned in Matthew 6:7 and being persistent in prayer?

7. What does it mean to "backslide"? How have you struggled with this in your own life?

8. In many Christian churches today, confronting a Christian brother or sister about sin is the last thing to be done, if it is done at all. Why do you think this is the case?

9. What are some of the problems you encounter when trying to establish and maintain a regular prayer time? What has helped you overcome those prayer hindrances?

10. What have you learned from this book that you can take with you as you continue to grow in Christ? Pray and thank God for these things?

The "BE" series . . .

For years pastors and lay leaders have embraced Warren W. Wiersbe's very accessible commentary of the Bible through the individual "BE" series. Through the work of David C. Cook Global Mission, the "BE" series is part of a library of books made available to indigenous Christian workers. These are men and women who are called by God to grow the kingdom through their work with the local church worldwide. Here are a few of their remarks as to how Dr. Wiersbe's writings have benefited their ministry.

"Most Christian books I see are priced too high for me . . .
I received a collection that included 12 Wiersbe
commentaries a few months ago and I have
read every one of them.
I use them for my personal devotions every day and they
are incredibly helpful for preparing sermons.
The contribution David C. Cook is making to the
church in India is amazing."
—Pastor E. M. Abraham, Hyderabad, India

Great studies from the Pastor's Pastor.

Experience deeper truth for deeper life with Dr. Warren W. Wiersbe, the internationally respected Bible teacher. Introducing a new series of Bible study books for a new generation of Christ's followers. Perfect for group or individual study, each book in The Wiersbe Bible Study Series includes interactive questions, stories, illustrations, and flexible formats. It's all the depth and riches of Warren Wiersbe's Bible teaching for a new generation of readers.

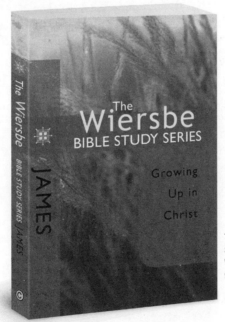

The Wiersbe Bible Study
Series: James
Warren W. Wiersbe
978-0-7814-4571-9

To learn more visit the David C. Cook
Web site or a local Christian bookstore.